RUNNING IN TRAUMA STILETTOS

THE BUTTERFLY PRESS
P.O. Box 260
720 Edison Furlong Road
Furlong, Pennsylvania 18925

eBook ISBN: 979-89872018-0-0
Paperback ISBN: 979-89872018-1-7
Hardcover ISBN: 979-89872018-2-4
Library of Congress Control Number: 2022919789

First Edition
Book Production and Publishing by Brands Through Books
brandsthroughbooks.com

Cover Photography: Brittany Breen, *www.brittanybreen.com*
The Butterfly Press Logo: Karima Neghmouche, *www.karimacreative.com*

www.whitneylynallen.com

RUNNING IN TRAUMA STILETTOS

A RAW GLIMPSE AT GRIEF AND LIFE AFTER LOSS

A MEMOIR BY

WHITNEY LYN ALLEN

CONTENTS

PRAISE FOR *RUNNING IN TRAUMA STILETTOS*

"Whitney Allen's *Running in Trauma Stilettos* does more than tell the story of how she tragically lost her husband. It's with unapologetic honesty and insightful humor that Allen offers us the chance to grasp the experience itself. Her memoir is a mosaic of memories, shared with such riveting details that one thing is clear: this is not a how-to-grieve manual, nor is it meant to document the journey of mourning. It is a glimpse into how we can find ourselves both unraveling and becoming a stronger version of ourselves in the face of unimaginable tragedy."

—Achilles Yeldell, author of *The Humble Opinion* and *Raised by the Bar*, a memoir

"In *Running in Trauma Stilettos*, Whitney Allen bares her broken heart and resilient soul over the tragic death of her thirty-five-year-old police officer husband, Ryan. Hers is an unvarnished message to others navigating unimaginable loss and paralyzing grief: There is light on the other side of darkness."

—Phil Gianficaro, former columnist for USA Today Networks

PRAISE FOR *RUNNING IN TRAUMA STILETTOS*

"If you are navigating a significant personal loss, this book will be the glimpse of hope you need to start embracing life again while still allowing yourself to grieve. I reached out to Whitney during my husband's journey with brain cancer, and we've stayed in touch to support each other now as two young, widowed mothers. Whitney tells her story with bravery and humor. She has been a guide for me as I navigate the emotions and challenges of widowhood. Her perspective on life and her ability to turn this traumatic event into something so powerful is moving and is a true gift to other grievers."

—Rebecca DiTore, widow, mother of two, blogger

To Ryan, my soulmate and now my guardian angel—You were the one who gave me wings and pushed me off the cliff so I could write this book. Thank you for loving me so exquisitely. Because of you, I'll always know my strength and my worth. Thank you for teaching me how to love and embrace life in such a beautiful way, how to go after my dreams, and how to laugh with abandon. The boys and I are so damn proud of you, and we miss you every moment of every day. I'll be seeing you, boo. This one's for you.

To Jackson and Leo—I know you are too little to understand how grateful I am for both of you. You are my two beautiful reasons to continue to live life with joy and passion and to keep smiling and laughing. Thank you for loving me unconditionally despite all my imperfections. You are brave, sweet, smart, and funny little boys. Mama is so proud of you, and I love you both so much.

To Karen and Morgan—Thank you for making it possible for me to survive the darkest days of my life and for providing laughter and hope despite everything. You two are my rocks, and I know Ryan is forever grateful for your complete and unconditional love for me, Jackson, and Leo. We have been through the fire together and survived. I am looking forward to many more moments of laughing so hard we cry, enjoying lots of cake, beer, and tequila shots, and forever talking about our love for Ryan. You are both true warriors, and I love you with all my heart.

And to you, my reader—I hope you find the strength and resilience within yourself to continue to live your life in the pursuit of beauty and magic no matter what life throws at you. My promise to you is that, at the end of any dark tunnel, there is a light.

INTRODUCTION

I'VE JUST DROPPED OFF MY FOUR-YEAR-OLD, Jackson, at day care. I'm sipping a venti iced Americano while sitting on a stool at one of the high-top tables at the Starbucks on Main Street in Doylestown, Pennsylvania. Except for my mismatched powder-blue sweatshirt and army-green workout pants, I look very normal and unassuming. But I'm not normal at all. I'm not waiting for a friend or passing the time while my oil is getting changed. I am at this Starbucks waiting for the funeral director down the street to text me that I can come and pick up my husband's death certificate, ashes, and blanket. The same blanket he was wrapped in when he was carried away in a body bag—dead at the age of thirty-five from an anoxic brain injury.

Even as I appear to be sitting perfectly still at this table, my entire body is vibrating, wanting to run as far away from my reality as possible. This is the dichotomy of my life right now—the fake smiling when I want to cry, the embracing hugs from strangers when all I want to do is tell everyone I'm touched out, and calmly talking about my husband's memorial when I just want to scream at the top of my lungs how unfair this all is.

I am now tasked with the unimaginable, with what seems impossible: beginning my lifelong trek as a widow at the young age of thirty-five, with two small boys to raise without their father. I have to walk, run, jog, dance, and prance in trauma and grief shoes, which I can only describe as trying to get around in the most hellish type of stiletto heels. These are the type of shoes you can't walk five feet in without getting bloody blisters. No one wants to wear these damn shoes. But, like Cinderella, they fit me perfectly, and I have been running a marathon in them since October 2021. The things I have experienced from the time of my husband's accident to today—the moments that are forever seared into my memory and haunt my soul—are the dark kind, the kind that no one likes to hear or talk about.

I wrote this book for all the young widows and mothers who, like me, have been in the dark crevices of life and know what it's like to step into hellish shoes you can never take off. This book is for all the people who have been through grief and trauma, who have had thoughts and feelings that scared them, and who felt no one else could truly understand. The stories in this book may not look exactly like yours, but I hope you can see yourself in some of them. Anger, frustration, fear, loneliness, resentment, trauma responses, guilt, sadness, even happiness, laughter, and hope are all things I have felt and experienced since my husband's accident in October 2021. This is not a how-to book but one that gives an unapologetic glimpse into the world of grief and trauma.

My hope for those who read it and have lived a charmed life—as I did for so many years prior to Ryan's accident—is that you will come away being able to better empathize with those who are going through some of the hardest days of their lives.

For those who have already endured the hardest days of their lives, this book is my way of saying, "I see you."

And for those who are reading this who are currently battling through the hardest days of their life, I know you feel like the biggest boulder has been placed on your chest, and you are begging for relief. I hope this book gives you the permission to feel and process your grief—in your own authentic way, without guilt or shame.

No matter where you are, my hope is that this book helps you see that you are not alone.

CHAPTER 1

THE DAY CAPTAIN AMERICA FELL

I WAS STARTLED AWAKE IN THE DARKEST hours of the morning on October 14, 2021. I'd had a nightmare that there was a creature, blackest of black, hovering over my husband of eight years, Ryan, as he slept. In my nightmare, I tried to scream at this creature to go away, but it didn't flinch. I remember feeling helpless as no sound escaped my mouth. In my nightmare, my mind recognized this creature as the angel of death. I sat up in bed and instantly turned to my left, where Ryan was sleeping peacefully. *It was only a bad dream*, I thought, as I lowered my growing, twenty-six-weeks-pregnant body back to the mattress. *Everything is okay*, I thought to myself. I focused on the sound of Ryan snoring softly next to me and examined his beautiful face in the darkness, slightly illuminated by the moonlight shining through the side cracks of our black-out blinds. Ryan's soft snoring was always calming to me, but as I drifted off back to sleep, I couldn't help but feel a deep foreboding in the pit of my stomach.

* * *

It was September 1, 2021, the first evening in many weeks that Ryan had off from work. He was a K9 officer with the Hatboro Police Department in Montgomery County, Pennsylvania, and often worked overtime during the summers when the rest of the department took their beach vacations. When everyone else was playing hard, Ryan would put his head down, making as much overtime as possible. It was important to him to provide the best life for his growing family. At the time, we were expecting our second baby boy in early 2022. I was relieved on this particular evening to have some help with our three-year-old son, Jackson, and I was excited to spend some time with Ryan since we had been passing ships for several weeks. But the universe had different plans.

This was the evening that multiple strong tornadoes hit the area, including the EF-3 tornado that hit Mullica Hill, New Jersey. Instead of spending family time together, part of the evening was spent in our very wet basement, crouched behind dilapidated cardboard boxes filled with old books and beer glasses. Ryan's ninety-pound German shepherd, K9 Louie, was also in tow, obediently sitting as Ryan and I watched the news on our phones to see the tornado's path. I frantically tried to find something on Jackson's iPad to keep him entertained as we waited out the storm. From where I was sitting, I could see outside the two windows across the room.

The sky suddenly turned pitch-black, the wind picked up, and the rain went from a consistent pitter-patter to sounding like buckets of water were being continuously thrown at the house. I looked at Ryan with obvious panic on my face as he walked to the other side of the basement to get a better look at what was happening outside. I thought to myself, *as long as Ryan's here, everything will be fine.* He had always been the brave, stoic, strong one in the relationship. I, on the other hand, was the dramatic and frantic one. I held Jackson tightly as he watched *Cocomelon* on his iPad, blissfully unaware of what was happening. The rain and wind finally let up, and the news confirmed what we already knew—the tornado had just passed us.

Then Ryan's phone rang. It was the station calling. "Hey, what's going on?" he asked the person on the other end of the line. I could hear the muffled sounds of a deep voice on the line while Ryan nodded his head. "Okay, I'll be right in." I instantly rolled my eyes after hearing that phrase come out of Ryan's mouth because on the one night that Ryan had off work, he was now having to rush into the station. "I have to go in to work," he said, looking at me earnestly with his hazel eyes. I crossed my arms and started shaking my head. Ryan looked at me and sighed. "The borough is flooded, and there are people stuck in their houses and people floating down the street in their cars. I have to go, babe." Now he sounded a little annoyed because he could probably sense I was about to give him shit for going in.

I had no say in the matter. Ryan always felt the undeniable desire to be the hero when he was needed. He thrived on the department asking him to help out in a pinch, and he knew on this particular night that he needed to go do water rescues. I was pissed off as all hell that our evening had not gone as expected, but I knew there was only one place Ryan would accept being on that evening. It was always hard for me to stay mad at Ryan. "I love you, boo," he said, and then he kissed me hard on the mouth and ran upstairs to get changed for his night at work.

Before Ryan left that night, I wrapped my arms around his torso like I always did, my face burrowed against his chest, his chin resting on my head. Ryan had turned into such a strong, physical presence in the ten years since we had met, going from a tall, skinny, one-hundred-seventy-pound young man to a two-hundred-twenty-pound, muscular, fit father and husband. I moved my hands up and down his back and felt his back muscles. I breathed him in and said, "Be safe, Captain America," a name Jackson had started calling Ryan after an episode where he had caught Jackson in midair before he tumbled down the stairs. The name had stuck, given that Jackson thought Ryan was a superhero and given that Ryan was a six-foot-two, all-American stud. The name was fitting.

I felt a little sick to my stomach that he was on his way in to work in such dangerous conditions, but after almost ten years together and being a police officer's wife for the majority of those years, I knew the deal.

Ryan came home late that night; I had stayed up and waited for him. He walked into the bedroom, soaking wet but with a big smile on his face. With the help of some other officers, he had been able to save several individuals from drowning. We stayed up even later so I could hear the heroic tales about his night. Eventually, I drifted off to sleep, relieved that the love of my life was safe in bed next to me.

* * *

On November 22, 2021, Ryan received a commendation for his heroism on the night of September 1, 2021, specifically for making several water rescues and saving many lives with the help of other officers from his department. Jackson and I accepted Ryan's commendation on his behalf. At the time, Ryan was completely incapacitated, with a severe anoxic brain injury. He was a patient in the Neuro Intensive Care Unit at Penn Presbyterian Medical Center, and he was fighting for his life.

* * *

It was 2:00 p.m. on October 14, 2021, and Ryan had just gotten home from a CrossFit workout. He greeted me with a big smile in my office on the second floor of our home, where I was sitting on the loveseat with my laptop on my lap, answering interrogatories for one of my cases as a medical malpractice defense attorney. He was on the phone with his best friend, Steve Plum Jr., a K9 officer from Warrington Township. "Okay, man, I have to go and talk to my wife now," he said, laughing. Nonchalantly, Ryan told me he had been stung by a bee on the car ride home from the gym. He lifted his arm and pointed to the upper part of the inside of his bicep where he had been stung. Abruptly, Ryan interrupted our casual conversation. "Babe, I feel weird," he said. His voice was full of fear, a tone I had never heard from him before. It stopped me in my tracks and sent chills down my spine. I threw my laptop onto the loveseat and swiftly stood my twenty-six-weeks-pregnant body up to go to Ryan.

"Can you breathe?" I asked, already tapping my phone screen to start dialing 911.

“I don’t know, babe,” he said anxiously. I ran into the hall bathroom to find Benadryl.

“My husband is having anaphylactic shock from a bee sting!” I shrieked into the phone to the 911 operator. I picked up and tossed various bottles around in the medicine cabinet, trying to find the Benadryl as I balanced my cell phone between my cheek and my chin. My hands were shaking. The bright-pink bottle finally caught my eye, and I pulled it out, knocking over several pill bottles. “God fucking damn it!” I screamed into the phone. I examined the bottle I had just grabbed from the medicine cabinet. “This is fucking children’s Benadryl!”

As I was on the phone with the operator, Ryan slowly hobbled down the stairs, his long and muscular arms stretched out, holding the railing on one side and the wall on the other, trying to balance himself, his back slightly hunched. Louie followed behind him quickly, almost slipping down the stairs, like he sensed the urgency of the situation. *This is bad*, I thought to myself.

“Ma’am, ma’am. I need you to calm down, please,” the 911 operator pleaded with me. “Do you know where your husband is right now? What is he doing?” I snapped back to reality. I had no idea where Ryan had gone.

“I don’t know where the hell he is!” I screamed into the phone. Realizing this was a much more serious situation than Benadryl could handle, I ran downstairs to try to find Ryan. I ran to the kitchen, looked desperately into our playroom, and then ran to the living room, searching for him. *Where the hell is he?* “Babe! Babe! Babe!” I screamed as I ran from room to room in my bare feet. I suddenly noticed that the front door was slightly cracked, and I flung it open to discover Ryan seated on our front step, slumped over like a rag doll, his broad shoulders protruding out. "Babe!" I cried as I ran to him.

"I found him!" I screamed at the 911 operator, my voice shaky and breathless.

"Okay, is he breathing? What is happening?" the operator asked calmly. Suddenly, everything around me melted away, and I was laser-focused on Ryan. He was struggling to breathe, his chest forcefully rising and falling as he gasped for air. I put one of my arms across his back and the other one on the back of his head as I attempted to lay him on his back. My arms and pregnant belly strained as I lowered Ryan's limp, two-hundred-twenty-pound body to the cold, stone porch. His head thumped lightly as it touched the ground.

"I don't know if he is breathing," I told the operator. "Fuck, fuck, fuck. Babe, stay with me, okay? You're okay. I'm here. You're okay, you're okay, you're okay," I tried to assure him.

"Okay, you'll have to start doing chest compressions," the 911 operator said in the most annoyingly calm voice. "Just count with me . . . 1, 2, 3, 4 . . ." I placed my right hand over my left hand, interlocking my fingers, and started forcefully pressing down on Ryan's chest.

"1, 2, 3, 4 . . ." I breathlessly repeated to the 911 operator. My voice cracked as I held back tears. "HELP! HELP! HELP! HELP ME!" I screamed. It was the most visceral and painful scream I had ever heard—the pleas of a woman whose world had just changed in an instant.

But the world around me didn't seem to notice. It was one of those warm October days that felt like summer. The air was thick, and the warm wind blew gently, the leaves rustling on the street. The bushes in my neighbor's yard slowly danced back and forth as my arms rhythmically pushed on Ryan's chest. Our usually busy neighborhood street was silent, empty. Like in my nightmare from that morning, it felt like my screams were just going into a dark abyss. I was helpless and petrified.

"Where are they?" I asked the 911 operator as I continued to pump on Ryan's chest. "1, 2, 3, 4 . . ." I repeated over and over in a hushed, breathless chant. I thought about running to get help, but I couldn't leave Ryan. I just had to keep doing what I was doing until help arrived. I continued to scream, pleading for someone, anyone, to help me, but I didn't see a soul. "Stay with me, babe. Please stay with me. I love you." Ryan was still trying to force air into his lungs, his eyes wide open, and foam started running from his mouth. "I think he's vomiting!" I yelled at the operator. I instinctively turned him on his side so he wouldn't choke on what was coming out of his mouth, then gently turned him on his back again and restarted chest compressions.

It felt like a lifetime had passed before I heard sirens in the distance through the thick, warm air. I felt a huge sense of relief wash over my body. "I hear sirens," I yelled to the 911 operator as I continued to count out loud and administer chest compressions to Ryan. A Doylestown police officer was the first on the scene, and he got out of his car and ran to the front porch. The ambulance arrived shortly thereafter. In all the chaos, I hadn't even noticed Louie outside. At this point, he was leaping back and forth like an antelope, clearly in distress.

"You have to get that dog under control!" the officer shouted at me in a stern voice. By this point, someone from EMS had taken over helping Ryan, so I jumped up to try to control Louie.

"I fucking know!" I screamed back at the officer as I tried to wrap my arms around Louie, who was frantic at this point. He didn't have a collar on, and he wouldn't budge from the spot where Ryan was lying.

I ran into the house, my bare feet making loud thumping noises on the wood floor as I made my way into the laundry room and grabbed the first collar I saw, neatly placed on the hanger where we hung Louie's leashes and collars. I ran back outside and straddled Louie as I clipped the collar around his neck. Then I yanked Louie in the direction of the open front door and flung him into the house with all my might, shutting the door hard behind me, Louie's stunned and sweet face on the other side. At this point, there were several people working on Ryan on the front porch. I saw them quickly and methodically set up the machine to shock his heart, and I ran off the porch and onto the driveway where Ryan's black Jeep was parked. I couldn't see exactly what was happening from where I was standing, and I couldn't bring myself to get closer as I heard, "Clear!" As they shocked Ryan, I saw his feet jolt up in the air and then fall back down to the stone front porch violently. It was all too much for me to bear.

One of the Doylestown police officers approached me as I paced back and forth. He started asking me a series of questions, and I instantly started clenching my fists and my jaw in frustration. *Why the fuck is he trying to talk to me right now?* I thought. I screamed something similar to him, and he looked me up and down and noticed my pregnant belly through my flowy, blush-colored, long-sleeved shirt. "Can you please sit down, ma'am? I really think you need to sit." I must have looked like a complete maniac or like I was going to pass out. He then looked me straight in the eyes and said, "Listen, I know this is a lot right now. I just need information from you to help your husband, okay?" He was kind and obviously worried.

"Okay, I'm sorry," I said. And I was sorry. I was completely out of my mind with worry about Ryan. As I paced back and forth in front of the police officer, still having no idea how Ryan was, I noticed my hands were shaking, and I interlocked my fingers, making a tight fist to steady them. "Is his heart beating? Is he dead?" I asked the police officer desperately. He turned away from me without saying a word and walked quickly toward the front porch, where the paramedics were still working on Ryan. My heart was beating so hard that I thought it would burst as I waited for news that I knew in my bones I didn't want to hear. The police officer turned back in my direction, looking down at the ground as he stomped toward me in his bulky, black work boots, his baton swaying rhythmically back and forth from his thick belt. I felt myself hold my breath.

"His heart is not beating, but they are working on him," he said so matter-of-factly that it shocked my entire system. I started to hyperventilate as I put my hand on the side of Ryan's Jeep and tried not to vomit or pass out.

A few minutes later, I found myself in the back of a police car on my way to Doylestown Hospital. We had left the house with Ryan's heart still not beating. I thought he was dead. In the back seat of that police car, I clasped my hands together and prayed. I prayed hard; I rocked back and forth with my hands against my lips, and I shut my eyes. "Please let his heart start, please let his heart, please let his heart start," I breathlessly whispered, pleading to a God I wholeheartedly believed in from my upbringing in the Jewish faith but that I hadn't ever really had to pray to before or ask anything of. But at this moment, I needed Him to show up in a big way. Unfortunately, I didn't know that God's answering my prayers would start the clock on the darkest days of my life.

We got to the hospital and walked through the big automatic doors of the front entrance of the emergency room. "Ma'am, do you have a mask? You have to put a mask on," the elderly security guard politely said to me. I just looked at him with blank, bloodshot eyes as I instinctively reached out my arm to take the stiff, blue hospital mask he handed me. I forgot there were still rules and people to enforce them. All I could think of was my husband, dead in the back of an ambulance on the way to the hospital.

"Why don't you wait here?" the police officer said as he led me to a corridor on the left side of the emergency room entrance. It was big and bright and airy. He left to get more information about Ryan and told me he would be back. I started pacing again. My hands found themselves in prayer, and again, I begged God to help Ryan, to start his heart, to make him be alive for me and the boys. I paced back and forth, and I prayed in that corridor until I saw the kind Doylestown police officer walking toward me. My heart started thumping in my chest again, and I thought I might pass out.

"They were able to get Ryan's heart started in the ambulance on the way here." He delivered the news with his hand lightly on my back to steady me. I instantly dropped to my knees and sobbed.

* * *

"You are truly a woman of valor . . . I am so proud that you are my daughter."

This was a text I got from my dad, Steve, on March 17, 2022, the day Ryan was put on hospice. My father's text was beautifully sad, heartwarming, and honest. He went on to talk about his own father's death and how cheated he felt by it, the same way I felt cheated by Ryan's eventual fate. At this point, Ryan's brain was beyond repair, and even the best medical advancements and rehabilitation in the world could not bring him back. It was very unlike my father to share his feelings so openly with anyone. In fact, he had never been open with me about his feelings my entire life, and he had never once talked about his father's death with me. My grandfather's sudden death from a heart attack at an early age in front of my father was an event that was traumatic and life-altering. My father had never dealt with his father's death or processed it, and it had affected how he dealt with situations and his emotions his entire adult life. It was a dark cloud that hovered over him at all times, and it was a taboo subject in our family growing up. But faced with Ryan's impending and inevitable death at a very young age, my dad felt the need to share a part of himself that he usually never shared. I cried as I read the text, so much so that I had to hand my phone to my mother-in-law, Karen, so she could finish reading it. It was also very difficult for my father to tell me he was proud of me. I actually don't remember another time in my life he had said those exact words, even with all I had accomplished. Those powerful words made me finally feel accepted by him after so long and after having a complicated relationship with him. After everything I had been through—all the pain, the heartache, the impossible decisions, all the battles I had fought throughout Ryan's ordeal—my father could finally see the woman I had become. That was a gift he gave me as Ryan was dying. It would be one of the few blessings during what was otherwise the darkest journey of my entire life.

CHAPTER 2
RYAN'S LAST RIDE

IT WAS EARLY JUNE 2022, AND RYAN HAD BEEN dead for two months.

I found myself hovering over my jewelry box in my room, staring at my engagement ring and wedding band, which I had worn proudly as Ryan's wife for eight years and seven months. I had made the conscious decision to stop wearing them the day Ryan died because those rings felt like they tied me to a different life. They were a symbol of the bond and commitment Ryan and I had made on October 12, 2013. When Ryan died, it was as if I felt that bond we had on earth disintegrate into a million pieces, like my body and soul just knew he was no longer here on earth to carry out the commitment we had made to each other. Those rings were also a symbol of a woman who had died the day Ryan died. I was no longer a wife, or even a caretaker, to my husband. I didn't belong to anyone anymore, and I felt it. I was free, but it felt uncomfortable. I liked belonging to someone. I loved belonging to Ryan.

I stared at the beautiful antique rings, the diamonds glittering in the light from the new lamp from West Elm I had recently purchased to make my room look like "mine" and not "ours." I picked up the wedding band first and slid it slowly onto my left ring finger; then, I did the same with my engagement ring. My hand and fingers looked different than when I had worn these rings before Ryan died. They looked leaner, longer, and stronger somehow. A little less feminine. I looked down at my hand with the rings and danced my fingers so I could see the light hit the diamonds like I had done so many times before, especially when Ryan and I had gone out to dinner, and I could appreciate them as I looked at my gorgeous husband across the table. There was always something about restaurant lighting that made my rings look extra sparkly. As I danced my fingers, I thought about how it felt to belong to someone for so long, with those rings as an outward symbol to the world, and then it suddenly felt like I had been punched in the gut. As I stared at the rings, I whispered, "Till death do us part." Then I quickly slid off the rings and placed them back in my jewelry box, where they would be displayed next to Ryan's wedding band. I decided that day that putting them on may not be the best idea. I thought that even if I belonged to someone else down the road, I would never belong to Ryan again. I would never be his wife again on earth, and that thought was devastating. I clicked off the lamp, still staring in the direction of the jewelry box, and left the room.

* * *

Ryan and I had gotten engaged in the most anticlimactic way. We took our relationship to the next level on a trip to New York City in the summer of 2012. It was morning, and we groggily looked at each other after a terrible night's sleep on a pull-out sofa belonging to one of Ryan's oldest friends and his wife. "Maybe we should get married," Ryan said in a matter-of-fact way.

"Are you joking? It doesn't sound like you're joking," I said, looking at him with a half smile on my face. At that point, we had only been dating for three months. But it felt right to call Ryan my fiancé. I was already his, and he was already mine. We didn't feel the need to be on anyone else's timeline. "Yeah, I think we should be engaged," I told him as I leaned in for a kiss. The city morning sun began to beam through the big window in the living room. It was decided; we were to be married. We didn't need a fancy engagement to validate our commitment to each other; a simple question on an early morning was all we needed. We were in love. It was as simple as that. I smiled to myself as I lay on that pull-out sofa in that tiny New York City apartment with the sun shining down on my bare legs.

We made the engagement official once we were back home in the suburbs of Philadelphia. We decided it was time to purchase my engagement ring, and we went to an antique store together so I could pick out my own. I settled on a ring set that included both an engagement ring and a wedding band from the 1940s that fit within our very tight budget at the time. The rings were simple but beautiful, and we exited the antique store excited, knowing this was the first big thing we had done as a newly engaged couple. As soon as the door to the antique store closed behind us, Ryan swiftly pulled out the ring box and proudly slid the engagement ring onto my left ring finger as we stood on the sidewalk. "I guess you're really stuck now," he said with his famously big smile. I laughed as I looked down at the ring that was now on my finger. Ryan could always make me laugh. It felt right to be his.

* * *

That evening of October 14, 2021, the day of Ryan's accident, he was airlifted from Doylestown Hospital to Penn Presbyterian Medical Center in Philadelphia. A preliminary CT done at the Doylestown emergency room had shown extensive damage to his brain. Ryan's attending physician at Penn, Dr. Michaels, was calm and frank as he explained Ryan's condition in the family waiting room of the Neuro ICU. He explained that the brain was complicated, and there was no way of knowing Ryan's prognosis at that time, but that Ryan was in a coma and was fighting for his life. Their main concern at this time was Ryan's brain swelling because that is the brain's natural response to deprivation of oxygen or to trauma. Dr. Michaels explained that brain swelling could lead to brain death and that their best way to monitor and thus control the swelling was to surgically place what is called a "bolt" in Ryan's brain that would continuously monitor Ryan's intracranial pressure or ICP. His team would then be able to administer the right cocktail of medications to hopefully prevent further damage. He also explained that Ryan stood the best chance of avoiding brain death if he was put in a state of hypothermia, cooling his body down to between thirty-two and thirty-three degrees Celsius and then slowly heating it back up to normal body temperature.

Dr. Michaels handed me a pile of consent papers as I sat, staring blankly at the wall in front of me. "Okay, let's do it," I said so matter-of-factly that I surprised even myself with the tone. I gently pulled the pen out of Dr. Michael's hand. *I can't believe this is happening*, I thought to myself as I signed my full name in neat cursive on the various lines, consenting to bedside brain surgery on my husband and putting him in a suspended state of hypothermia. As a medical malpractice defense attorney for nine years, I had read, analyzed, and summarized thousands of pages of medical records, taking in every meticulous detail of a stranger's medical history to properly defend a lawsuit. But I was too shocked, traumatized, exhausted, and scared to read every word of these consent forms. Instead, I flipped through the pages, and words like "death," "hemorrhage," "stroke," and "brain death" flew out at me. *This is the only way to save him*, I thought. But I was freaking out on the inside. *I'm thirty-four years old. I'm not supposed to be having to make these life-and-death decisions for my husband! We are having a baby soon, for Christ's sake!* I screamed in my own head. As I finished signing all the consent papers, I felt dazed, but the growing baby in my belly suddenly kicked me furiously, bringing me back to reality. I had felt in a dream state since Ryan's accident, and the baby's kicks were a harsh reminder that life moves right along, even if the worst possible thing happens. "Whitney . . ." My mother-in-law's voice brought me even further back into reality. Karen had just heard the exact speech I had from the doctor, and she looked shell-shocked. Karen had always been a force to be reckoned with. She was intense as all hell and didn't need anyone to help her navigate through life. She and Ryan's father, Pete, had a very turbulent relationship. They separated when Ryan was a teenager, and Pete passed away when Ryan was in his early twenties. In many ways,

Karen was very used to navigating life's challenges with limited support. Over the ten years Ryan and I had been together, Karen and I grew very close. I was lucky to have a mother-in-law with whom I got along so well. But this was the first time I had ever seen her vulnerable and without a solution. "Michael is going to your house to pick up anything you need. What do you want from home?" Michael was Karen's first cousin, and I had known him since I first met Ryan and had built a strong relationship with him. Michael and Karen were extremely close, so much so that they were often mistaken as husband and wife. "Please tell Michael I just want Ryan's wedding band from his jewelry box," I answered. "It should be sitting right on top."

Several hours later, Michael arrived with Ryan's wedding band. I wanted something tangible of Ryan's to have close to me at all times, to be able to touch, hold on to, and focus on while I prayed hard at Ryan's bedside. I put my hands around my neck, gently unclasped the necklace I was wearing, and carefully slid Ryan's wedding band onto the chain with the other charms. Now heavy with the weight of Ryan's white gold wedding band, I raised the chain back up to my neck. The ring lay flat and heavy against my chest. It was beautifully and carefully carved with a paisley pattern, Ryan's favorite. I twirled the ring between my thumb and pointer finger.

I wore Ryan's wedding band around my neck through his seven-week admission to the Neuro ICU at Penn Presbyterian, his first admission to Moss Rehabilitation in Elkins Park, his month-long admission to a long-term acute care hospital in Bethlehem, Pennsylvania, an eight-week admission to Moss

Rehabilitation for therapy for the second time, through making the decision to put Ryan on hospice instead of continuing his therapy, and then finally, through twenty-two days of hospice before Ryan died on April 7, 2022.

* * *

It had been a few days since Ryan's accident and his admittance to the ICU at Penn Presbyterian in critical condition. Ryan's best friend and K9 officer at Warrington Police Department, Steve Plum Jr., offered to bring Ryan's K9, Louie, to the hospital to see me during one of my twelve-hour days there. Steve loved Ryan like a brother and cared for our family like his own, so he wanted to do anything to bring us some distraction or joy. I immediately agreed, believing Louie was my connection to Ryan and home, a place I had not been in days. I was living in a place five minutes from the hospital just in case Ryan's condition continued to deteriorate. I was desperate to hold onto my old life before the afternoon of October 14, 2021, crushed all my hopes and dreams for the future, and I thought Louie was a chance to feel closer to what I had known and loved. I was sitting in one of the large leather chairs in the lobby of Penn Presbyterian when I turned my head and saw Louie coming down the long corridor. He was so amped up he was practically running on the slick, white tile. Steve was bracing and leaning back as much as he could to reduce Louie's speed, and it looked like he was getting dragged by a one-hundred-pound wolf. People darted to both sides of the hallway to avoid Louie, who was panting and slobbering, obviously stressed by the new and odd environment he found himself in. I got up from my chair and started moving in their direction. "Louie!" I cried, not even trying to hold back my tears. I hurried toward him, and he greeted me with his tail wagging and lots of wet dog kisses. I kneeled down to the ground as best I could, given I was twenty-seven weeks pregnant, and I buried my face into his thick neck as hot tears rolled down my face. I wanted my old life back. The life where I should have been watching my husband and son play outside on our swing set while Louie happily ran in the yard. Instead, here I was, terrified to leave the hospital because I didn't want my husband to die without me present. I could hear Ryan's and Jackson's laughs in my head as I thought of the family memories that had occurred just several days prior. In the moment, I was so grateful to see Louie, but I had never felt further away from my old, beautiful life prior to October 14.

* * *

On March 17, 2022, ten years to the day that Ryan and I had met and fallen in love at first sight, Ryan was transferred to hospice. It was the beginning of the end, which only made me think more about our own beginning. Ryan and I meeting for the first time had been serendipitous, perfectly and elegantly coordinated by forces that cannot be seen or understood. I was in my second year of law school at Villanova, living at home with my parents, who were going through a very messy and contentious divorce. I was freshly single, having left a long-term relationship that had ended badly several months prior. I had vowed to "work on me" after my breakup, focusing on my studies and hobbies. Ryan was also recently out of a long-term relationship that had ended badly. He was a cadet with the Montgomery County Police Academy with my sister Rachel and living at home in Quakertown, Pennsylvania. Rachel had invited her classmates to our childhood home to pregame before going out to the bars in Manayunk to party and celebrate St. Patrick's Day. At the time, I was a mostly retired and reformed party girl after four years of undergrad at Syracuse University. The last thing I wanted to do was get out of my pajamas and be social. But on that night, something in my gut told me to put on a dress and heels and march my way down the stairs to join Rachel's academy friends for a night out. I decided to wear a formfitting white, black, and teal dress I had borrowed from one of Rachel's academy classmates. I carefully straightened my short blonde hair, and I even applied makeup for the occasion. I walked into my parents' kitchen, and there was Ryan, standing behind the black granite island with a big smile on his face. He was tall and thin. He had not quite matured into the man he would grow into, but he had a very handsome face and the brightest smile I had ever seen. His laugh filled my parents' kitchen. It almost echoed it was so loud.

He looked up right away as I walked into the kitchen, trying desperately not to trip in the heels I was no longer used to wearing. A lot of people may think love at first sight is reserved for the movies or television, but I can say for certain that it exists because that is what happened with Ryan and me. We locked eyes the moment I entered my parents' kitchen, and it was like the entire rest of the room and all the people in it just melted away. It was just us, gravitating toward one another—like we had no choice in the matter. Although it was not the perfect time to be meeting someone new for either of us, I couldn't ignore my immediate attraction toward Ryan and the way he made me feel. He made me belly laugh with his witty banter, and when he took my hand to hold it on the taxi ride to Manayunk, my entire body felt chills. We talked, laughed, and kissed all night long, acting like we had been in a relationship for years. It was like my soul already knew him. It felt right to be with Ryan, like our meeting and falling in love had been planned from the beginning of time. Little did I know that ten years to the day that we met, I would be having to watch Ryan, my husband of eight years, start hospice, where I knew he would take his last breath and where death would part us.

The thing is, even if I had known on that fateful St. Patrick's Day in 2012 that I would only have Ryan for ten years, I would have chosen him over and over again.

* * *

Ryan was transferred from Moss Rehabilitation to Michael's house in an ambulance wrapped with the American flag and followed by a huge and beautiful police procession called Ryan's Last Ride. We had chosen Michael's house for Ryan's hospice so Ryan would not die in the place our sons were growing up in. I knew Ryan would not want Jackson to associate Ryan being sick and dying with the place he felt the safest and most comfortable. Michael loved Ryan like a son and offered his house to avoid this potentially traumatizing scenario. It was the most selfless thing anyone had ever done for our family. Ryan's Last Ride included hundreds of police and K9 officers from across Pennsylvania and New Jersey riding in their police cars and on their motorcycles. It was something I had only ever seen in the movies or on television, and I was awestruck by the entire event. Along the route, children in schoolyards were jumping up and down with huge smiles on their faces and signs that read: "We Love Officer Allen." Citizens from all across Montgomery and Bucks counties waved American flags as they cheered and waved. Doctors, nurses, and other medical staff came outside of Abington Hospital on Ryan's route home to pay their respects, many of them with tears in their eyes. I made sure that one of the locations on the procession route was Jackson's day care. As we drove through the parking lot, all the children were cheering and holding up signs for Ryan. At the end of the line was my brave little boy, Jackson, with a sign for his daddy with a big red heart and a blue line through it. Jackson wore his favorite Buzz Lightyear jacket for the occasion. He looked so happy and proud that the huge police procession was for his daddy. Prior to the event, I had prepared him by telling him that we would be going through his school's parking lot with a big line of police cars driven by Daddy's friends because Daddy was special. As we passed the day care, none of the officers could hold back their tears, and neither could I. It was the most amazing spectacle I had ever seen, and it was for Ryan, my beloved and amazing husband. I was so damn proud. Ryan had always been so humble and never believed that he was very likable. He could come off as rough around the edges, but to know Ryan was to love him, and he was the most loyal and trustworthy friend and colleague. I thought how sad it was that Ryan would never know the overwhelming impact he had on an entire community. I wished that in heaven, Ryan would learn of everything that had happened while he was sick and that he would realize just how loved he truly was by so many. Ryan's Last Ride was his epic homecoming after five months of hellish hospital and rehabilitation admissions. I was so happy for him that his next and final stop was the ultimate destination—heaven. He would finally be free.

CHAPTER 3

THE MESSIAH LOVES ADELE

"SO, WHO'S GONNA TAKE ONE FOR THE TEAM?" I asked my sister-in-law, Morgan, and my mother-in-law, Karen. It was November 2021, almost Thanksgiving, and we were sitting in the sunny and warm lobby of Penn Presbyterian Hospital. It had been a little over a month since Ryan had been admitted to the Neuro ICU. Ryan had avoided brain death, but he was still in a coma and on a ventilator. My laptop was on my thighs, in front of my expanding pregnant belly, as I continued what seemed to be the never-ending journey of attempting to figure out the best way to pay all the monthly bills and balance the checkbook, a task Ryan had been solely responsible for during our ten-year relationship. He would often joke that if anything happened to him, I would be "absolutely screwed" because he had done all the administrative and financial tasks to keep our household going. I hated to admit that in the moment, I felt he had been right. I was absolutely screwed trying to figure this all out on my own. At that point, I had already spent many hours on the phone with different companies explaining to them that my husband couldn't come to the phone because he was in a "fucking coma," and I had appropriately given myself the nickname of "the scary pregnant lady." I was heading toward the brink of a mental breakdown when my mother, Debbie, happily pranced down the long corridor toward where Morgan, Karen, and I were sitting.

"Here comes the Messiah. Can someone please explain to me why she always looks so fucking annoyingly happy?" I said under my breath to Morgan and Karen. Morgan and Karen knew the deal: I could not be alone with my mother for more than a few minutes, or else I would completely go off the rails, especially now, when my patience was at an all-time low, and my anxiety was at an all-time high. I ironically called my mother the Messiah to everyone but her because, in her mind, she believed when she made her appearance, it was like some sort of Second Coming, and everyone should welcome her with open arms. I was irked by her toxic positivity, passive-aggressiveness, complete lack of self-awareness, and inability to read a fucking room. We had been estranged for many years and had not spoken or seen each other for over a year prior to Ryan's accident. Now here she was, frolicking down the hallway of Penn Presbyterian to visit Ryan, who was still in a coma, trying to insert herself into our trauma bubble. My parents had been divorced since 2013, and my eccentric lawyer father, Steve, had shown up to the ICU with his briefcase and computer so he could check his stock portfolio and answer work phone calls. Both my parents lacked some emotional intelligence, so I didn't have high expectations of them. But my dad tried his best to show up in a supportive way. He would be present but only capable of talking about the stock market, gushing about his plethora of dogs, or complaining about his new wife. Through Ryan's ordeal, my dad did the best he could—checking in with the occasional text, call, or visit—and I was grateful for that.

My mother, on the other hand, found Ryan's incapacitated state to be the perfect time to take advantage and attempt to get back into my good graces, thinking I would be at my weakest without Ryan by my side. In fact, I was being even more obsessive about protecting my peace, and I felt like a sleeping dragon waiting to breathe fire on anyone who pissed me off, including my mother. During Ryan's six-month ordeal, there were only a few people who had been openly welcomed into the trauma bubble, the original members of which consisted of me, Karen, Morgan, and my brother-in-law John. Strict boundaries had been set almost immediately, given the complexity and intensity of the situation. There was just not enough time, space, or energy for others to enter the bubble, and most people were not able to handle the darkness that enveloped its members.

"I'll go upstairs with her." Morgan exhaled the words with a huge sigh. She knew she would instantly regret that decision to sit in Ryan's hospital room with my mother, but she also knew I just couldn't mentally handle my mother on my own.

Morgan and I had grown very close over the years. She was stoic, smart, and clearheaded. But she also had the biggest heart of anyone I knew. Plus, she had one hell of a sarcastic sense of humor—one of the main reasons we got along so well. She was equal parts badass and sensitive, which I appreciated so much. She had been my rock after Ryan's accident and was often the person I turned to for sound advice, clarity, and comfort.

"Taking one for the fucking team!" I joked as my mother pranced closer to our chairs. The Messiah was upon us. "Hey, little mama!" my mother exclaimed. "How is everyone doing today?" she asked with a huge smile plastered on her face.

"We're fine, Mom. Morgan is going to go up with you to see Ryan today, okay?" I didn't need her permission—I just needed her away from me.

"Okay . . ." My mother's voice drifted off like she was disappointed I wouldn't be sitting with her in Ryan's room. Morgan slowly got up from her chair and swung her bag over her shoulder. She had a work call she had to be on, so at least she wouldn't have to actively engage with my mother in Ryan's hospital room. Morgan started walking toward the elevators to the fifth floor and the Neuro ICU. My mother followed behind Morgan. Her short blonde hair and five-foot-one, one-hundred-pound frame made her resemble a child as she hurriedly tried to catch up to Morgan, who was speed-walking toward the open elevator doors.

"Godspeed," I said out loud to no one in particular as I continued to punch numbers into my phone calculator.

Morgan texted Karen several minutes after she and my mom had gone upstairs. "Oh, dear Lord," Karen said under her breath after reading the text.

"What's happening?" I asked, full of curiosity and dread.

"Apparently, your mom found a medical article that said playing Adele's "Rolling in the Deep" has woken people up from a coma, so she is playing it very loudly up there in Ryan's room," Karen explained.

"What in the actual fuck?" I managed, as I started laughing hysterically. "Poor Morgan . . ." I continued to laugh so hard I had to wipe tears from my eyes. It felt good to have a reason to laugh again, even if it was because my mother was being an absolute lunatic in the Neuro ICU at Penn Presbyterian. "You know, if Ryan does wake up from his coma soon, my mother really is going to think she is the Messiah, with the power to wake people up from comas." I couldn't help myself; I was laughing uncontrollably at this point, picturing my little blonde mother up in the Neuro ICU blaring "Rolling in the Deep," bopping around, with Morgan looking absolutely horrified, trying to concentrate on a work call. My mother couldn't help but make everything about herself, even my husband's tragedy. *Ryan is missing all the good stuff*, I thought with a sharp, deep pain in my heart. For the last ten years, Ryan had been my person—the person I confided in, laughed with, and cried with—the first person I would tell if something ridiculously funny happened. He knew every detail about my family and all their idiosyncrasies, and he would fucking love this story. The problem was he was the only one I couldn't tell it to.

CHAPTER 4

SPREADING ASHES AND DIGGING GRAVES

IT WAS SIX WEEKS AFTER RYAN'S DEATH, THE DAY that would have been his thirty-sixth birthday—May 21, 2022. We were painfully tasked with trying to figure out how to honor Ryan over his birthday weekend instead of celebrating with him. It was the first of Ryan's birthdays without him on this earth, and the grief was all-consuming. Karen, Morgan, John, and I decided we should spend the weekend doing some of Ryan's favorite things. That meant eating spaghetti and meatballs, drinking a lot of craft beer, and spending time on the water soaking up the sun with my two sons, four-year-old Jackson and four-month-old Leo. It was also what we felt was the perfect time to spread the majority of Ryan's ashes in the ocean: his favorite place and a representation of his eternal freedom from illness and pain. It was the final act of love we could provide for what remained of his physical body after months of caring for him as a family.

Our first attempt on Saturday, Ryan's actual birthday, to spread his ashes was, in true Allen fashion, a complete shit show. We drove out to the spot where Ryan, Jackson, and I had spent the last Fourth of July weekend waterskiing, tubing, and hanging out with Morgan and John. To this day, that weekend remains one of the most special and fun times of my entire life. It was the epitome of perfect family time. I was newly pregnant with Leo, and Ryan and I stared at each other knowingly throughout those two days, not saying a word but knowing exactly what the other was thinking: we had built a beautiful life together. We were content and grateful, and I was blissfully unaware that the next time I would be on the same boat would be to spread Ryan's ashes and say my final goodbyes.

"Does anyone have a screwdriver?" Morgan asked as she examined the bottom of the loaner urn we were given by the funeral director for Ryan's memorial. We were prepared to spread Ryan's ashes in the ocean, unaware the urn was sealed with screws.

"You're joking, right?" I asked, already knowing that Morgan was most definitely not joking.

"Well . . . that sounds about right," Karen said, chuckling to herself.

"Why don't we try opening it with a bottle opener or a bottle cap?" John suggested, who was always trying to make life easier for the Allen women, which we usually made extremely difficult for him to accomplish. John took a bottle cap from one of the beers we'd been drinking, bent it in half, and attempted to coax the first screw loose from the bottom of the chestnut urn. It was useless; the screws on the bottom of the urn were on so tightly even John's muscular arms couldn't make them budge.

"We could throw the entire thing in the ocean. I mean, the funeral director said we could keep the urn," I half joked, but the idea of taking my little boys on another boat excursion the next day seemed daunting. I was exhausted.

"We can't do that. Then Ryan will be trapped in there forever," Karen said. She was right, of course, and we all agreed to take the boat out again the next day to properly spread Ryan's ashes, this time unscrewing the urn before going out.

The next morning was overcast and cooler than the day before. I decided to leave Leo with our nanny at the house while the rest of us went out on the boat. *It is so like Ryan to want to get another fun day out on the boat*, I thought. It was like he had arranged for us to be caught by surprise by the screws on the urn the day before, like he wanted to spend one more night with his family under the same roof and go on one more boat ride and enjoy the sun, wind, splash of salt water, and buzz of the boat engine. It was just like Ryan to draw out the fun. We were all quieter on this day, naturally spent from the roller coaster of emotions from the previous one. I sat in the back of the boat and just let all the emotions come as we sped off toward our final destination. I looked up at the sky and saw that the clouds were billowed together like hundreds of cotton candy sticks stuck together, in all shades of white and gray, with a small opening that was perfectly surrounding the sun. I noticed then that the opening in the clouds was in the shape of a heart, as if Ryan had painted the sky that day, reminding us that he was with us and forever watching over us from the heavens. I felt that familiar lump in my throat as tiny droplets of salt water splashed themselves on my face.

John turned the boat engine off as Karen pulled out the chestnut urn again for our second attempt at spreading Ryan's ashes. This time, we made sure we would be able to accomplish our mission. Karen pulled out the plastic bag, where Ryan's ashes were tightly packed. The ashes were a beautiful white color, like ground-up seashells, and I thought to myself that, even cremated, Ryan was still the beautiful boy I had loved since the first day I had laid eyes on him. Although I knew in my heart that Ryan was already gone, I had to steady myself to say goodbye to what was left of his physical life here on earth. It was another terribly sad thing we had been tasked with, but certainly not the worst.

"Who wants to do it?" Karen asked Morgan and me.

"I'll do it," I said as I reached out my hands to take the plastic bag from her. *It could only be me*, I thought. I climbed over the back of the boat to the swim platform, holding Ryan in my right hand. I stood facing the water, bobbing gently back and forth as I untied the bag and opened the top carefully. "I love you, boo. Ashes to ashes, dust to dust," I whispered to myself, cradling the bag in my open palm as I slowly tipped it over the water. I watched the first batch of white ashes touch the water. They lingered on the top of the water for mere moments and then disappeared beneath the tiny waves. I continued to tip over the plastic bag, and more ashes poured out into the water beneath me until the bag was completely empty. I held the bag completely upside down for a couple of seconds and noticed a few more tiny white particles fly into the air. *The hell is finally over,* I thought to myself. *Ryan is free, and so am I.* I felt waves of despair but also relief and peace as I stared at the empty bag where Ryan's ashes were once housed. I resumed my position in the back of the boat. Jackson snuggled up next to me, with his feet up on the seat, and nestled his little head, which housed his beautifully thick, dark-brown hair just like his daddy's, into my chest. John started the boat engine, and we sped off into the open water in front of us. It was time to go home and start my new life with Jackson and Leo without Ryan, and I was ready.

* * *

I sat quietly in the gray chair next to Ryan's hospital bed and stared in a trance at the two large monitors on either side that were keeping track of all Ryan's critical bodily functions, including his heart rate, blood pressure, and respiration. It was October 2021, and Ryan had been admitted to the Neuro ICU at Penn Presbyterian for a little over a week, being kept alive on a ventilator, his body being cooled slowly by a machine to promote healing in his brain. Ryan's condition was touch and go, prompting several phone calls in the middle of the night from his medical team informing me that Ryan's intracranial pressure (ICP) was rising to higher-than-normal levels, and they were having trouble controlling it with medications. With each ICP crisis, Ryan was inching closer and closer to brain death and further from ever being able to come home. The truth was that Ryan was hanging on by a thread, and his physicians had absolutely no positive news to share other than the fact that he was still alive, barely.

The prior evening, the fellow on Ryan's case, Krupa, had walked into Ryan's hospital room and caught me in a rare moment by myself. She sat down next to me and sighed a deep sigh before telling me to "prepare myself" and suggesting that I "get my affairs in order" as it was very likely Ryan wouldn't make it past the critical couple weeks after suffering an anoxic brain injury. I was thirty-four years old and twenty-seven weeks pregnant with a three-year-old at home. I thought to myself, *how is this my fucking life?* I nodded my head methodically as she delivered news that no one should ever have to hear about the love of their life, especially one that was thirty-five years old. I looked over at Ryan after Krupa left and cried hard. I muffled my cries by pushing my entire face into my forearm, which was leaning on the hard rail of the hospital bed, and I prayed to God to take me instead of Ryan. The pain of the thought of losing him took my breath away as I listened to the hiss and clicking of the ventilator forcing air in and out of Ryan's lungs and the high-pitched beeps of all the machines surrounding me. Ryan still managed to look so damn handsome, even with tape wrapped around his entire head, keeping the machine measuring his ICP in place. Finally, I managed to get my shit together because I knew what I had to do next: I had to deliver the news to Karen, Morgan, and John, who were waiting for me in the lobby downstairs. I exited Ryan's hospital room in a complete daze and walked down the hallway of the Neuro ICU, glancing every so often at my reflection in all the glass panes that surrounded me, my pregnant belly so prominent now. I walked into the elevator and hit the button for the lobby with the feeling that I was watching myself from above, like in a movie, and not like this was my actual life.

"Krupa said we need to prepare ourselves. She thinks there is a very significant chance that Ryan doesn't make it," I said, choking back tears. Everyone stood up to embrace each other, with no words left to say between us. There was only sorrow, despair, and death surrounding us like a dark cloud, and we all felt suffocated by it. We held each other tightly in a big circle and sobbed. Our cries were the only sounds in the quiet lobby of Penn Presbyterian that night while Ryan lay unresponsive in his hospital bed on the fifth floor.

The next afternoon, I found myself sitting in the same gray chair next to Ryan's hospital bed, chugging down a Starbucks venti iced coffee. I was so exhausted. I was analyzing Ryan's vital signs (my new hobby) when Karen swiftly walked into the room with her arms full of bags. Her face also showed the exhaustion we were all feeling, but she looked stunned and fucking over it. "Kitty is dead and is now buried in my backyard," she said very matter-of-factly as she attempted to place her bags on the free chair next to me. "Jesus Christ, Karen, I'm sorry. What the hell happened?" I felt terrible, but I was also desperate to hear any story to distract me from my reality. Karen sat down next to me in Ryan's ICU room and explained in detail what had happened to her cat, Sandy, whom everyone called Kitty.

The day before, Karen had gotten a call from her neighbor who was watching Kitty while Karen, Morgan, John, and I stayed at an Airbnb five minutes from Penn Presbyterian to be close to Ryan. The neighbor told her, "Kitty doesn't look well." She hadn't been eating or drinking, and her plump body was rapidly losing weight. Karen's neighbor took a picture of Kitty to send to Karen, and she immediately knew Kitty was ill. Karen had gone home the night prior, after being told to "prepare ourselves" for Ryan's death, to a dying Kitty. It was the cruelest joke from the universe—a big fuck you. And after a full week of being in the ICU with Ryan and the emotional roller coaster we had been going through, the sleep deprivation, and now a dying Kitty, Karen broke down.

* * *

John volunteered to take Kitty to the vet the next morning while Karen made her way to the ICU at Penn Presbyterian to basically sit in a vigil at Ryan's bedside based on my conversation with Ryan's fellow the night prior. Tests performed at the vet showed what Karen already knew. Kitty was dying. Specifically, she was having kidney failure, and extraordinary measures would only prolong her life, not save it.

"Okay, so Kitty is in kidney failure," John informed Karen over the phone. "So, what do you want to do here? Do you want to be with your son or with your cat?" Ever since Ryan's accident, John had been the glue keeping me, Karen, and Morgan from the brink of breakdown. He asked how we were doing, gave us extra-long "John hugs," and made sure we were fed. More specifically, he made sure I had an appropriate stream of baked goods as a stressed-as-hell pregnant woman. He had been flawless in his execution to keep the Allen women as calm as possible in crisis, except for a mishap when he handed me a raisin muffin that he mistakenly thought was chocolate chip. I told him I was disappointed and convinced that baked goods should never come in raisin form. The hospital cafeteria was surely playing a sick joke on me. John took everything in stride and had even driven me all the way from the hospital back home to Doylestown when I was in no condition to drive myself. John was a saint, and now he was tasked with a dying Kitty.

“Well, that is a hell of a choice,” Karen had said to John over the phone. She decided to go to the vet to say goodbye to Kitty and put her down. Karen arrived at the vet and walked into the exam room, where Kitty was lying comfortably on the metal bed, purring. John tried to comfort a hysterical Karen as Kitty was put to sleep peacefully, but John was just as inconsolable. A potentially dying Ryan and now a dead cat was too much emotional bullshit to take in a week.

* * *

Karen and John walked out of the vet’s office with dead Kitty in a plastic bag. “We have to dig a grave now,” Karen told John as they walked to their cars. Once they got to Karen’s house, they made their way to the backyard, to the same spot where Ryan’s cat Max was buried under a chestnut tree, with a shovel and pickaxe in tow. John began hitting the hard ground with the pickaxe, and Karen began shoveling away the soft dirt to make a deep grave for Kitty. Karen and John took turns using the shovel and the pickaxe to secure a safe burial. The grave was finally deep enough to satisfy Karen, and Kitty was placed in the ground. Karen and John finished dumping all the unearthed dirt over Kitty’s final resting place. To ensure that no animals would dig her up, Karen and John rolled a block of cement over the loose dirt. Now sweaty and covered in dirt from grave digging, Karen turned to John over Kitty’s grave and said, “Okay, so we killed the cat, buried the cat, and now back to the ICU.” She headed back to the house with the shovel in her hand as John followed behind with the pickaxe. That day, I endearingly named John “the dirty jobs guy.”

CHAPTER 5
DO LAST RITES EXPIRE?

RYAN HAD BEEN ON HOSPICE FOR TWELVE DAYS when we finally decided it was time to let go. It was March 28, 2022, when Ryan's family and I decided he would stop receiving any nutrition or hydration except for what was needed for his comfort medications. We had been struggling to face this decision because we knew it meant beginning the process of the inevitable—that Ryan would die. None of us could bear the thought of letting him go after six tortured months of doing everything in our power to keep him alive in the hope he'd recover. Making the mental shift from saving Ryan at all costs and being his caretakers to letting him die was excruciatingly painful. But after imaging of his brain performed at Moss Rehabilitation had shown that the parts of Ryan's brain that made him who he was weren't even present anymore, we knew there was only one choice. Ryan wouldn't have wanted to live without any real life in him, more helpless than a newborn child, on display in a hospital bed with other people changing his diaper, with no ability to know where he was and who was surrounding him, with no ability to feel or process emotion, laugh, cry, or move any of his limbs. Ryan was a proud and stoic man, and I knew in my heart of hearts that allowing him to die with dignity was the most decent thing I could do for him, for the man I had been in love with every day for ten years. Ryan's feeble, helpless physical body was the only thing left of the once strong, loving, funny, and brilliant man who'd existed prior to October 14, 2021. But all of these rational reasons for allowing Ryan to die made it no easier on us. It was the single most gut-wrenchingly painful decision I have ever made in my entire life.

* * *

Ironically, on the same morning we made the decision to stop his nutrition, Ryan's feeding tube was clogged. It was the nudge we needed to stop all of Ryan's life-sustaining measures. We were all terrified and didn't know what the process would actually look like. He was to be kept as comfortable as possible through the process of starvation and dehydration, which we were told would lead to his body completely shutting down, with a cocktail of hospice medications, including ample amounts of Ativan, morphine, oxycodone, and Haldol. I prayed that it would be a quick and painless transition for Ryan but also for our family. Little did I know the sheer agony that awaited us in the next eleven days. Three days after stopping Ryan's feeding tube and hydration, he was already showing signs of decline. His urine output dropped drastically, his heart rate increased rapidly, and the time between his respirations began to elongate alarmingly. By late evening, we were told Ryan's condition had made a turn, and it likely would not be long until he passed. I had been preparing myself for this next part for weeks since the topic of hospice was privately discussed between Morgan, Karen, and me for quite some time before we had even announced it to the world. However, I had quietly known in my gut for even longer that Ryan was gone, and he would never be coming home to me and our babies.

Later that evening, I climbed into the rickety hospital bed next to Ryan and lay next to him. It was the first time I'd been able to since the morning of his accident, October 14, 2021. I put my head on his chest. There were no more tubes or monitors hooked up to him and no feeding tube to avoid tugging on or pulling out by accident. I thought this was the end, and I wanted to feel and hear his heartbeat for the last time, the heartbeat I so intimately knew. I listened to the rattle of his chest with every labored breath he took, not realizing I was holding my own breath, waiting for each one to be Ryan's last. As I lay waiting for Ryan's heart to stop, my ear pressed up against his chest, I noticed I could feel and see every bone in his body. Ryan had become a shell of himself since October, and with no nutrition or hydration, his skin looked suctioned to his bones.

* * *

The cavalry arrived soon after we made some phone calls telling the essential people that Ryan was close to the end. We called Ryan's friend from high school, Ben, who is an Episcopalian priest and who agreed to perform Ryan's last rites; Ryan's best friend, Steve, and his wife, our very dear friend, Nancy; and Drew Valleley, Ryan's sergeant, mentor, and friend at Hatboro

PD. It was well into the late evening, and Ben, Steve, Nancy, and Drew all entered the threshold of Michael's house with the same look of dread and sadness on their faces, their eyes glassy, likely from crying during their respective car rides. Each of them gave us big hugs as we all gathered around Ryan's bedside, still waiting for him to die. It was a blessing that on this particular night, Jackson had passed out on the mattress we were sharing upstairs, and baby Leo was fast asleep in his Pack 'n Play crib. Ryan's respirations were still few and far between when they all settled around Ryan's bed. "Do you want me to perform the last rites?" Ben asked with some hesitation and so much kindness and understanding. Ben knew how difficult this was for all of us and the absolute hell we had been through the last six months.

I turned my head and looked at him. His eyes looked pained that he was having to perform the last rites for one of his dearest and oldest friends. "Yes, please," I told him. I'm Jewish, and Ryan wasn't even religious, but it felt right. I knew Ryan would approve of Ben, who had married Ryan and me eight years prior, performing Ryan's last rites before his journey to heaven. I climbed out of Ryan's hospital bed, my right side now completely numb, and went to sit in the folding chair next to the hospital bed so Ben could perform Ryan's last rites. I held back tears as I watched Ben slowly open his Bible and begin reciting:

> *Into your hands, O merciful Savior, we commend your servant Ryan. Acknowledge, we humbly beseech you, a sheep of your own fold, a lamb of your own flock, a sinner of your own redeeming. Receive him into the arms of your mercy,*

into the blessed rest of everlasting peace, and into the glorious company of the saints in light. Amen. May his soul and the souls of all the departed, through the mercy of God, rest in peace. Amen.

"Amen," everyone said in unison.

The moment was beautiful, sad, and heavy. Big, hot tears quietly streamed down my face as I continued to watch Ryan's chest rise and fall. We all waited and watched Ryan for what seemed like an eternity. But instead of continuing to decline, Ryan began to rally. His respirations increased, his color turned from gray and ashen to a healthier red and pink, and his heart rate stabilized. "Okay, so this isn't happening tonight?" I looked around at everyone's faces, just in awe that we had all prepared ourselves for Ryan's death, except it appeared that Ryan wasn't quite ready to go. I stood up from the very hard and uncomfortable folding chair and made my way to the kitchen. I felt so emotionally and physically drained and frustrated that this nightmare felt unending and relentless. I was even angry at Ryan for not dying and being so damn stubborn. This anger quickly got turned toward myself for wanting the whole thing to just be over after six impossible months. I suddenly felt an intense wave of guilt wash over me as I made my way to the refrigerator and opened it. My eyes darted right to the beers illuminated by the interior light, and I carefully examined the alcohol content of each one. I decided that chugging a high-alcohol-content beer and getting somewhat of a buzz was the only way to get through this fucked-up night. Being only three months postpartum, chugging a strong beer usually did the trick. I popped open the bottle and took several big chugs of a Belgian-style ale as I stood in front of the kitchen island and stared at the wall in front of me. I took a few deep breaths and decided to walk back into Michael's formal living room to rejoin what we ironically called "Happy Hospice," where everyone was gathered. Soon, we all joined in the drinking, eating, yelling, and storytelling around Ryan, who was on his deathbed and drugged to high heaven. The night that we all thought was Ryan's last night had suddenly turned into a fucked-up death party, and a raucous one at that.

At some point, it was decided that the fucked-up death party needed sad cake and lots of it, which is exactly what it sounds like—cake you eat when you're sad. I had eaten a lot of sad cake the last six months. In fact, the ritual had taken on new life during Happy Hospice and had become something everyone knew about. Different cakes, pies, cookies, and various assortments of baked goods were constantly showing up at the door of Happy Hospice, where the doormat appropriately read: "Welcome to the Shit Show." Some friends came back from the grocery store with lots of sad cake, including a chocolate peanut butter one, which is one of my favorites. Someone in the group also decided to take out the leftover barbeque that was in the fridge because why the hell not if everyone was here and no one was dying? I was too exhausted, devastated, and sickened over the night's events to protest. I continued to chug my beer in silence, sitting in the folding chair next to Ryan's hospital bed.

Several hours went by, and after everyone had their fill of food and alcohol and it became clear that no one was dying that night, the room started to quiet down. It was time to wrap up our fucked-up death party and get ready for another day in the "bubble of despair," as we liked to call hospice. I started to get up out of that horrible folding chair next to Ryan's bed when it occurred to me that Ben was leaving for vacation and that Ryan might die while he was gone. "Hey, Ben, just curious, since you're going on vacation and everything, and you may not be here when Ryan actually dies . . . do last rites expire?"

He laughed and confidently said, "No, they don't."

I got up, put the back of my hand on Ryan's cheek, and gently stroked it back and forth, looking at his sweet face. "Good night, babe. I love you." I then said goodbye to the remaining people in the room and dragged my exhausted and now buzzed self up to bed so I could be a little less zombie-like for "death watch" the next day.

* * *

It was early March 2022, and Ryan's scheduled discharge from Moss Rehabilitation after two months was imminent. His mother, Karen, and I were training with the physical therapy team to learn how to care for him. The plan at that time was to take Ryan home after discharge and continue his rehabilitation to the best of our abilities. We were tasked with learning everything about his care, which was 24-7 and included medication administration and feeding through his J-tube, tracheostomy care, including learning what to do if Ryan's trach came out, turning and repositioning him, changing his diaper and changing his clothes, mouth care, transfers, and physical therapy exercises. Ryan was completely dependent and fragile, requiring almost constant care and management. He was a shell of his former self, and staring at him in his wheelchair on this day, knowing how strong, capable, and vibrant he once was, broke my heart. I was devastated that after everything we had been through, after all the miracles on this hellish journey, including Ryan being brought back to life, Ryan's ending could not be changed, and he would never be himself again. He was pale and thin, and due to his brain injury, his beautiful hands curled into themselves, and his wrists had become contracted. Ryan's eyes were open, but they mostly looked up into the air, and he had a permanent look on his face of complete unknowing and unawareness. At times, his eyeballs would quickly move from side to side, which was another consequence of his severe anoxic brain injury. His mouth hung open, and large amounts of drool often escaped. We carried gauze and paper towels with us so we could clean all the saliva from Ryan's face. Ryan's trach was so loud on that day. It crackled and popped as thick mucus moved through the tube, often causing him to cough violently and look like he was struggling to breathe.

Karen rubbed Ryan's arm as he sat in his wheelchair, and the physical therapist explained all the care that was required to manage Ryan at home. It was completely overwhelming, and as I heard her rattle off all the tasks that had to be done in a day just to keep Ryan alive and out of pain, I knew in my heart that Ryan would never want to live this way. Karen began sobbing as the physical therapist continued her spiel, unfazed by our tears. Karen eventually walked out of the room to gather herself. Although it was unspoken between us at this time, Karen also knew that Ryan's journey was coming to an end and that keeping him alive this way was not an option. There was no way in hell Ryan would want to be kept alive just to be on display. He wouldn't want to be bedridden, with his wife and mother caring for him. Ryan wouldn't want his sons to grow up in a household with a sick father who couldn't actually be a father. I cried uncontrollably in this moment because I knew all these things were true so deep in my bones that I was shaking as I stood staring at my very sick husband. I knew exactly what Ryan would want and what he wouldn't want, and that meant I had to let Ryan die with dignity. The only option for Ryan and our family was to put Ryan on hospice and let him go, to give him the ultimate peace and freedom. *We are done here. It's over,* I thought to myself as tears continued to stream down my face. I looked at Ryan in his wheelchair, the physical therapist still talking away. While on this earth, Ryan would never be healed and whole again. Although it pained my soul, I knew what we had to do next.

CHAPTER 6
BRAVE LITTLE BOY

"I JUST WANT JACK TO BE PROUD OF ME," RYAN SAID to me in bed one night, out of the blue, referring to our three-year-old son, Jackson. It was summertime, just a few months before his accident that would take place in October. The comment caught me off guard, like Ryan knew something I didn't. It gave me chills. I tried to shrug off the weird feeling that washed over me, and I said reassuringly, "Babe, of course he is proud of you. You are his favorite person, and you're like a real-life superhero. How could he not be proud of you? Not to mention you also have plenty of time to make him proud . . ." My voice trailed off then. Ryan said that same comment to me several more times before his accident, almost like he was pleading with me. Each time, I became more curious and worried about why he was saying such a thing over and over. The comment turned out to be prophetic. I didn't know it at the time, but I truly believe Ryan somehow knew deep in his bones that he would be leaving a legacy for his sons rather than being able to raise them with me. His comment was preparing me for this impossible inevitability; it was preparing me for the fact that part of my job as a parent without Ryan would be to teach our boys about how amazing he was and to give them every reason to be proud of the man, husband, and father he was.

* * *

"You just have to wear the mask until we get to Daddy's room. Okay, babe? Just a little bit longer, I promise," I said as I corralled Jackson up to Ryan's ICU room, with Karen and Morgan following close behind. It had been an entire month since Jackson had seen Ryan on the morning of his accident. Ryan had just undergone a tracheostomy and a G-tube placement, so his face was no longer bombarded with various tubes down his throat. I felt it was time to give our three-year-old son some context to me constantly having to say, "Dadda is very sick; he is in the hospital, and doctors are taking care of him and trying to make him better." Each time I said those words, I felt like I wanted to vomit. It made our hell of a situation real, and it felt so unfair and unjust, especially for our son, who certainly didn't deserve having his father ripped away from him. We pleaded with Ryan's physicians at Penn Presbyterian to allow Jackson the opportunity to visit, even though with COVID protocols, technically, no one under twelve was allowed to visit patients in the Neuro ICU. One of Ryan's attending physicians pulled some strings, and we were granted permission to have Jackson come see Ryan before visiting hours one Sunday morning. It felt like a small act of mercy for our family, given what we had endured in just four short weeks. My heart pounded in my chest as the elevator doors opened. *What if Jackson is scared of Ryan? What if this is just too much for him?* My thoughts felt slightly panicked as I slowly inched toward the elevator doors. It was too late to second-guess my gut feeling that this was the right decision for both Jackson and Ryan.

Jackson hated elevators and started to make a beeline in the opposite direction down the long corridor of Penn Presbyterian. "I don't want to go in the elevator! I'm scared," Jackson pleaded with us.

"Jack, it's okay, babe. It's like a spaceship," I hollered after him, the annoyance and frustration in my voice hard to hide. He wasn't buying it, and my now thirty-weeks-pregnant body wasn't mobile enough to chase a speedy, defiant toddler down the hallway.

Morgan ran after him, wrapped her arms around his little waist from the back, hoisted him up, and carried him like a sack of potatoes toward the elevator that I was holding open. "It *is* like a spaceship. We are going to have so much fun riding on the spaceship!" Morgan reassured Jackson.

Thank God for them, I thought to myself. If I didn't have Karen and Morgan there with me through this whole ordeal, I don't know what I would have done.

Morgan carried Jackson into the elevator, and Karen pushed the button for the fifth floor. "Wow, wow!" Jackson said as the elevator jolted awake. It was the comic relief we all needed in that moment, and we all laughed at Jackson's reaction to the elevator. Once on the floor of the Neuro ICU, the front desk attendant, who had now become our best friend, buzzed us all in without us even having to announce ourselves.

I held Jackson's little hand as we made our way down the hallway to room twelve, where Ryan was. Jackson was dressed for the occasion in his Iron Man Halloween costume. "Your costume will make you brave, right little man?" I said to try to ease Jackson's hesitation, which was written all over his face as we made our way down the hallway and into Ryan's room. We entered the room, and Ryan was lying in an upright position in bed. He was handsome even in this fucked-up situation, and it looked as if he could just open his eyes at any moment and say, "Hey, babe!" I snapped back to reality as Jackson stared at Ryan with a half smile on his face. "Look, Jack-Jack, it's Dadda! You want to go over and say hi?" I tried to be as cool, calm, and collected for Jackson as I could muster, but I felt that familiar lump in my throat letting me know that tears were coming. I swallowed that lump down hard and thought about how brave Ryan was, how much he had gone through to even be alive right now, and how he would want me to be brave in this moment for our son. I took a deep breath in the surgical mask I was wearing and suddenly felt braver, as if Ryan's strong and courageous nature was being channeled through me. Jackson shook his head hesitantly at my question, like he was trying to make sense of all the new sights, scents, and noises.

Jackson crept toward Ryan's hospital bed, and I watched in awe of this beautiful boy we had made together and raised for the past three and a half years. Jackson didn't seem scared or upset, just curious and happy to see Ryan. "Dadda's not waking up. Wake up, Daddy!" Jackson said to Ryan in his sweet little voice.

"Hey, buddy, why don't you show your daddy the action figures you brought? I think he would like that," Karen said. Jackson got an excited look on his face like that was the best idea anyone had ever thought of and scurried to the basket he had filled with his Buzz Lightyear and Hulk action figures. He clashed them together like they were in battle. "Hey, Jack, would you want to sit on Daddy's bed for a little bit?" Karen asked. Jack nodded his head in excited agreement. I lifted Jackson onto Ryan's hospital bed, holding him out as best I could to avoid hitting my expanding pregnant belly in the process, and placed him between Ryan's legs, avoiding any cords or wires.

"Hey, bud, do you want to lie down and watch some YouTube on Daddy's phone and relax for a bit?" Jackson smiled and nodded as I handed him the phone. Jackson reclined back with a sweet smile on his face and lay comfortably between Ryan's legs. The room was quiet except for the sound of the video playing on Ryan's phone, the familiar sound of the click, hiss, and beeping of Ryan's ventilator that was now hooked up through his throat through his tracheostomy, and all the beeping machines that surrounded his bed. Jackson looked at me with his bright eyes and then went back to happily watching his video. I smiled softly and sat down in the gray chair next to Ryan's hospital bed. I rubbed Ryan's arms as I watched our sweet, brave little boy.

In that moment, I felt so proud of Jackson for treating Ryan no differently than he did before his accident, just like his daddy. The lump in my throat reemerged, and my eyes suddenly welled with tears at the thought that Jackson may never get his daddy back—or at least a daddy who was whole, a daddy who was able to play with him, run with him, laugh with him, and dance with him—all the things that were Ryan and Jackson's special things. This time, I didn't try to swallow the lump down; I just let my tears slide down my face as I looked at the top of Jackson's little head as he lay in the hospital bed with Ryan: his favorite person in the world.

* * *

"I just don't want to fuck up my kid, you know?" I said to the child psychologist on the other end of the computer screen, nearly five months after Jackson's first hospital visit. I sat on the sofa in Michael's TV room, and as usual, Karen and Morgan were right there with me. It was the end of March 2022, and Ryan was on hospice. We were being counseled on the best way to approach Jackson with Ryan's impending death. We wanted to make sure we did everything in our power to do right by a sweet little boy who loved his daddy so much. I feared saying or doing the wrong thing in terms of explaining Ryan's death to Jackson and wanted to bring in whatever help I could to navigate this unimaginable task. We were told to be as literal as possible when explaining to Jackson what was going to happen to Ryan in the upcoming days. I had to somehow articulate to a four-year-old that his daddy and hero would no longer be sick but would be dead, and the thought of explaining this to my child was excruciatingly painful. Karen and Morgan wanted to support me in this hellish endeavor, and they both came home with me to put Jackson to bed one night during hospice. Jackson automatically knew something was up since I was usually the only one who put him to bed. Karen and Morgan attempted to look nonchalant by talking to Jackson about the stuffed animals in his room and what pajamas he wanted to wear, but Jackson was too smart and knew this was not a typical evening. I felt sick to my stomach as I read Jackson's allotted two books for the night, trying to go over in my head exactly what I was going to say to my sweet boy and the best way to deliver it. I feared I would break down in tears and that I would scare him, but I told myself that Ryan would want me to be brave for our son. So, as I shut the second book and placed it on the nightstand, I took a deep breath and started the hardest conversation I have ever had in my life.

"Hey, Jack. Before we go night-night, I need to talk to you about something important, okay sweetheart? I need you to try to be a good listener, and if you have any questions, I want you to ask me, okay? So, you know how Daddy has been really sick and in the hospital with doctors trying to make him better? Well, the doctors told us that Daddy can't get better, so Daddy is going to die. Do you know what dying means?" I asked, looking directly into Jackson's fierce, deep-blue eyes. He shook his head, so I continued. "Dying is when someone's body doesn't work anymore. A person's heart stops beating. They don't breathe anymore, and they can't move, talk, laugh, sing, or dance. So that is what is going to happen to Daddy, and Daddy can't come home. Before Daddy dies, you can spend as much time with him as you want. You can sit with him, hug him, kiss him, talk to him, and say goodbye at Uncle Michael's house. I think Daddy would really like it if you did that. And Jack? I want you to know that you'll always have someone to love and take care of you and your brother, okay? I love you so, so much. Everything is going to be okay; I promise." I felt as if I had said all of that in one breath. It seemed as if I was watching myself from above while my body delivered this soliloquy to my son. I finished with, "Do you have any questions that you want to ask about what I just said?" As I held back tears, waiting for Jack to respond to my question, I finally came back into my body. My heart thumped rapidly in my chest, and a lump developed in my throat. I looked up at Karen and Morgan, who were sitting across from me on Jackson's bed. They were also waiting anxiously for Jackson to say something. But no words came. Instead, Jackson buried his head into his pillow and his favorite stuffed animal, a lion named Laffy. I was letting Jack take the lead, and he didn't want to talk about what I had just told him about Ryan. I understood too intimately how impossible the reality of our situation was, and I felt that Jack understood the gravity of what I'd just told him, although he could not or would not express it. I tucked Jackson's Spiderman comforter over his precious little body and just under his chin as he snuggled Laffy close and sucked on his two fingers to soothe himself. I bent down and kissed Jackson's forehead lightly, stroked the top of his head, and brushed back his thick brown hair. My job wasn't to force him to talk about the impossible but rather to leave all the options open for him when it came to how he wanted to approach Ryan's death and say goodbye to his daddy forever. I clicked off the fox lamp on the nightstand and made my way out of Jackson's bedroom as Karen and Morgan followed behind me, closing the door.

CHAPTER 7

LEO JOSEPH ALLEN

I WAS STARTLED AWAKE BY THE SOUND OF LEO crying in the next room. I had just drifted off to sleep after another long day of hospice, watching and waiting for Ryan, once the most vibrant man I have ever known, to die. Leo was just shy of three months old. Now, edging closer to the end of Ryan's life, the boys and I were living at Michael's house, where Ryan was on his deathbed in the formal living room. Jackson was sleeping next to me on a mattress on the floor, his legs diagonal and draped over mine. I was so tired that every bone in my body ached, my eyes barely cracked open to look at the baby monitor, and my shirt was damp with breastmilk. "God fucking damn it," I said into the darkness. I was just so tired. I wanted this whole nightmare to be over. I didn't want Ryan to die, but I knew it was the only way he could be free and at peace after months of suffering. And it was the only way out of this fucking hellhole of a life I was living, full of sadness, grief, pain, and anxiety.

I waited to see if Leo would settle. I couldn't even will my body to move. His cries became more intense with each second that I didn't go to soothe and feed him. "God fucking damn it," I repeated as I hurled myself out of bed and onto my feet. I stumbled around to find my phone so I could have some light in the next room. I walked into the hallway and onto the cold wood floor. I heard the soft and sickening buzz of the machine downstairs used to suction secretions from Ryan's tracheostomy. I hated that awful machine and the way it made Ryan grimace with pain every time. I had seen it done hundreds of times and shivered in horror each time. I crept into the room where Leo rustled around in his Pack 'n Play, screaming at this point. I turned the flashlight of my phone on and balanced it against a pillow on the bed so it illuminated the back wall ever so slightly. I picked Leo up by his armpits with his legs dangling, sat down on the floor, and pulled up the side of my shirt to nurse him. Finally, there was some silence as he began suckling. I rested my elbow on my knee and pressed my forehead into my palm. I closed my eyes and started rocking side to side.

In that moment, I resented having a new baby. The baby I begged Ryan to have to give Jackson a little brother or sister. The baby I was so excited to bring into the world *with* Ryan. One of the most beautiful babies I had ever seen. I resented it because it meant I had absolutely no freedom to feel what I should have been feeling. I couldn't focus on the fact that Ryan was dying because I had to keep track of a nap schedule, remember the times I needed to pump or nurse Leo to keep my milk supply up, and be up at all hours of the night to care for him alone in the darkness. On that hard floor in the house where my husband was actively dying down the stairs from where I sat, I resented the baby we had made together in love because this wasn't how it was supposed to be. I even resented Ryan for dying and leaving me to deal with it all by myself. There was no one else to nudge in the middle of the night to help feed and soothe the baby. I felt alone and like the worst wife and mother in the world for having these thoughts, but they came naturally as so many emotions flowed through my body. What kind of person resents their newborn baby and dying husband? The cruel and harsh reality of being a single mother to two young boys and raising them without a husband felt heavy and devastating on that floor as I continued to rock side to side, hot tears streaming down my face, with Leo now asleep at my breast.

* * *

It was January 8, 2022, the day I had been dreading for almost three months since Ryan's accident. The day I was scheduled to give birth to our second son, Leo, but without Ryan by my side. I should have been excited to welcome our second baby boy into the world, looking forward to the newborn bliss that you feel right after having a baby, looking forward to seeing Ryan become a father for the second time, and looking forward to seeing Jackson as a big brother. My heart should have been bursting at the seams with gratitude and happiness that Leo was going to make his grand entrance into the world on this particular morning. But instead, I felt nauseous. My heart felt like it had sunk deep into the pit of my stomach. I felt dread, anxious as all hell about the operation I had to undergo as well as the recovery, and absolute despair due to Ryan's absence. To add insult to injury on the occasion of giving birth without Ryan, I had tested positive for COVID just five days prior, so I knew I would likely test positive when we got to the hospital. That would mean extra restrictions, precautions, and complications. As if I needed anything else to deal with in that moment. I asked Morgan to be my support person since I couldn't imagine anyone else who could keep their shit together and keep me calm and humored in a high-stress situation—besides Ryan. I knew in my heart that Ryan would want Morgan to be there for me. It was my way of having a part of Ryan with me at Leo's birth.

* * *

"So, I guess I'm having a baby," I said to Morgan hesitantly, trying to keep my voice from shaking and trying to keep myself from completely losing it as I started to walk out of my hospital room, holding the back of the hospital gown closed so I wouldn't flash anyone. I tried to bring humor to the fucked-up situation that I found myself in at Doylestown Hospital. I walked down the long corridor of the maternity unit to the operating room, where mere minutes later, I would be lying flat on my back on a metal slab, being cut open in a room filled with the brightest fluorescent lights you can possibly imagine. In another cruel twist, I had to leave Morgan behind in the hospital room. Morgan had taken a rapid COVID test at home that morning, which came back negative, but an additional test at the hospital came back positive. This meant she couldn't be in the operating room with me. I found myself not only having to give birth without Ryan but having to give birth without anyone, and there was nothing I could do about it. I tried to hold back tears as I shuffled down the hallway by myself in fresh blue hospital socks, feeling baby Leo kicking my side and knowing it was the last time I would feel his little kicks from inside my belly. I thought to myself that Ryan would want me to be brave, and even though he wasn't physically present with me, I knew he was there with me in some way. I thought of all the things he would say to me if he could, and I could hear his voice in my head so clearly as I continued my journey to the operating room to have our baby. *Boo, you got this. You and Leo will be perfect. I love you. Don't be afraid.* His voice in my head sounded so comforting and confident, just what I needed at that moment. Ryan always knew the perfect thing to say to make me feel better, to make me feel safe and loved. Nothing about the last few months had been fair or easy. Before Ryan's accident, when we first found out I was pregnant, we were told our baby had more than a 50 percent chance of having a severe condition that wouldn't be compatible with life. Now, here I was, all alone, about to give birth to our odds-defying baby. But my connection with Ryan and our love for each other was so deep and powerful that it transcended this entire ordeal. I could hear his voice in my head, guiding me and supporting me through every hard decision, every fucked-up situation, and every twist and turn this journey led us on. Even unconscious and in a hospital bed, I felt Ryan's soul with me on the day of Leo's birth, and I trusted that he had my back like he always did.

* * *

I sat on the edge of the cold metal table in the operating room, hugged a pillow as hard as I could, and leaned over so the anesthesiologist could administer my spinal tap. I knew the drill from my first C-section, but this time, Ryan wasn't waiting in scrubs on the other side of the operating room door to join me at my side. It was just me and a number of physicians and nurses buzzing around the operating room and shouting things to each other over my head. *I can do this,* I thought. I braced myself for the pain of the needle being jabbed into my spine by closing my eyes and holding my breath. The drugs in the spinal tap act fast. So, after the anesthesiologist was finished, I was told to quickly swivel my legs around and lie on the metal operating table. I lay back and stared at the ceiling, wishing for it all to be over, for Leo to be safe in my arms, and for me to be healthy and back in the recovery room, nursing him and cuddling skin to skin. I tried to wiggle my legs up and down to see if the spinal tap had kicked in as the nurses put a curtain across my chest so I couldn't see my doctor cut me open and pull baby Leo out. My legs started to feel heavy, and I could feel the doctor pinch me to make sure I was numb enough to start operating. I tried to focus on my breath and thought about Ryan. I tried to pretend he was there next to me, smiling and cracking jokes like he would have if he had been there. The nurses tried to make small talk with me, but I was too focused and scared to even engage. I think they got the picture because they quickly stopped trying. "Okay, we are ready to start. Are you all set, Whitney? We're gonna have a baby!" my OB said excitedly.

I wished I had an ounce of excitement in my body at that moment. I just wanted to fast-forward through that part, the part where I was being cut open alone and scared because this baby had to come out. "I'm good!" I shouted into the space above me, trying to sound as convincing as possible and trying not to break down before she started to operate. I tried not to think about all the bad things that could happen while they were cutting me open, like bleeding out on the table and leaving both my boys parentless. I tried not to think about something horrible happening to baby Leo, but all I knew at the moment was tragedy. Those dark thoughts flooded my mind and knocked on my door like old friends who couldn't be stopped. The only thing I could do as I lay there helpless on the operating table and my OB cut a deep, horizontal line across my previous C-section scar was stare up at the fluorescent lights above me and think about life, death, and Ryan.

* * *

"I feel everything," I said, turning to the anesthesiologist. I remember from my first C-section that I felt a lot of pressure when they were trying to pull Jackson from my belly, but I didn't feel any pain. But this time, my spinal tap wasn't strong enough, and with every push and pull by my OB, I winced in pain and held my breath. I felt every contortion of Leo in my belly and every tug. It was terrible. The anesthesiologist promptly gave me another hit of whatever drug cocktail they had on hand, but I kept feeling every single thing my OB was doing. To make matters worse, it felt like she was having trouble pulling Leo out of me. I tried to focus on anything else but how my body was feeling in that moment. I tried to focus on seeing my beautiful baby, hearing him cry, and knowing that he was safe, that he was earthside, but all I could think about was how much it hurt. I clenched my teeth and jaw together. I went to itch my arm—I had developed cholestasis during Leo's pregnancy, which causes terrible itching. The anesthesiologist didn't realize I was itching because of the cholestasis rather than the narcotics. Quickly and without telling me, she gave me a dose of Benadryl. I was instantly drowsy and dizzy. "I don't feel right," I said to the nurse and anesthesiologist. I was furious that I was so fucked up, and I had to force myself not to pass out. I didn't want to miss the birth of our son because no one else was here, and no one would be able to tell me about it if I fell asleep on the operating table. I forced my eyes open with all my might as my head swayed back and forth, trying to keep myself from falling asleep from the Benadryl. "He's here!" my OB yelled from the other end of the operating table. I waited for a cry, any noise to signify Leo was healthy. It seemed like forever before he started screaming. As soon as he started crying, a huge wave of relief rushed through me. He was here and safe.

"I want to see him. Please, I want to see my baby," I begged, as I was high as a kite on Benadryl. After everything I had been through, all I wanted was to hold my newborn baby and feel him against my chest. But I wasn't allowed to because I had tested positive for COVID. Instead, I heard Leo's cries at the other end of the operating room, and I knew that he just wanted his mama, that he was looking for me, and I wasn't there. "It's okay, sweet boy. It's okay, it's okay," I said as loud as I could muster through my drowsiness so Leo would hear my voice. "It's Mama, Leo. I'm here, I promise." I choked back tears. It would take approximately an hour while I was in the recovery room for the hospital staff to finally allow me to hold Leo, our miracle baby. Leo Joseph Allen, named after his daddy, Ryan Joseph Allen, was born on January 8, 2022, at 1:08 p.m. Our perfect baby boy and the spitting image of his daddy.

* * *

"I really want this," Ryan said to me in the kitchen one evening after we had been told that due to the results of preliminary screening, the baby I was carrying had a very significant chance of having a debilitating, possibly fatal, genetic condition. It was mid-July 2021. The kitchen was dark except for the backlighting of our cabinets. Ryan was getting ready to take his K9 Louie out for a walk, and he was standing near the door to our basement. His face looked soft and worried. Ryan was usually so confident and sure of things in life, but in that moment, I felt his vulnerability and the fact that he knew he had no control over this particular situation. It made my heart sink, knowing that this was something I couldn't fix, that I couldn't make better for him. We were both devastated and scared. We had to wait and endure a series of tests before we knew for sure what was happening with our baby.

"I know, sweetheart. I want this, too," I said lovingly. We had been given an envelope with the gender of our baby by my OB's office and had opened it that day. Through tears, I had pulled out the paper, which revealed a picture of a baby boy lying in a hammock with a blue border that read: "It's a boy!" A moment that should have been very happy and exciting had been tainted by fear of the unknown. Ryan had really wanted another boy, a little baby brother for Jackson. I, on the other hand, had been certain it was a girl because of how sick I was during my first trimester. But Ryan would say jokingly to me, "I know it's a boy because you wouldn't disappoint me." It made me laugh every time he said it. But Ryan was right; we were having another boy. Except, I had to stop myself from picturing Jackson meeting his baby brother for the first time or playing with him. I had to stop myself from imagining outings as a family of four—me and my three beautiful boys by my side—because we didn't know if that was a possibility, and it pained me to anticipate a good outcome when the odds were against us. I walked over to Ryan and wrapped my arms around him, putting my head against his chest. "It's gonna be okay, babe. We'll get through this together," I said, trying to convince us both. Ryan rubbed my back and held me in his strong arms. We silently comforted each other, not knowing if the baby boy growing inside my belly that we both wanted so desperately would be part of our family's future. Looking back at everything, the synchronicities and signs throughout the entire journey, I believe that as Ryan held me in our dimly lit kitchen that night, he made the most selfless deal you can with God. He would give his life for his son's, and God accepted.

CHAPTER 8

GANGSTER JEW GETS THE WALMART SPECIAL

MY HEELS CLICKED FURIOUSLY ON THE HARD laminate floor as I rushed toward the venue's private room at Ryan's memorial service to make myself a drink. It was April 28, 2022, just shy of 1:30 p.m. We had been receiving people at Ryan's memorial for close to two hours. I had finally reached my limit of patience after receiving Ryan's aunt and uncle. They were the only close family members who couldn't bring themselves to see Ryan and say their goodbyes while he was dying on hospice. They gave the excuse that "everyone deals with this type of thing in different ways," and when I heard that, I couldn't roll my eyes into the back of my head far enough. Ryan had a relationship with them his entire life. We had been to family events with them for ten years, but when Ryan was dying, they didn't show up. There was no do-over here. I thought about how upset Ryan would have been at their cowardice. Ryan always showed up, especially for the hard things, because he knew that was when it really mattered. Ryan knew that showing up for the hard times in life is what defines you as a person and that just showing up when things were easy was a cop-out. But that was the type of man he was, the honorable type, the farthest from a coward you could get.

Thankfully, Ryan's other aunts and uncles had been present throughout all of Ryan's hospitalization, rehabilitation, and hospice. One of Ryan's aunts would sit and read to him, and another would sit by his bedside and tell him all about what was going on with the family and sing to him (which brought me to tears). One of Ryan's uncles made us grilled cheese sandwiches and tomato soup during hospice and sat with us for hours on end at the hospital, even when he didn't know what to say, not for any other reason than just to be there. These family members didn't shy away from the hard shit; they leaned into it. They didn't have to show up, but they inserted themselves into the darkness as willing participants, and I loved and appreciated them for it. They embodied the meaning of family when life gets really hard. Something I learned so intimately through Ryan's ordeal is that the status of "family" is earned. Some individuals had earned it, and others had sadly squandered that title beyond repair.

To add insult to injury, while in the receiving line of my husband's funeral, Ryan's aunt had the audacity to complain to us about the traffic from Florida in order to attend the service. Yes, the fucking *traffic*. While to my left was the love of my life in a box next to his picture, a folded American flag, and a flower arrangement. I cut her off as I looked at her with daggers and said as calmly as possible, "I can think of worse things." Ryan's uncle had a look on his face that showed he knew how inappropriate his wife was being, but he didn't say anything. I promptly turned my back on them and walked toward the private room where I knew sips of vodka were available and waiting for me. I pushed the green velvet curtain that separated the large, tented venue space from the private area to the side and went directly to the table where the alcohol was to pour myself a drink and steady my hands, which were now shaking with anger.

* * *

We had been in some sort of purgatory for a while, but a little over two months after Ryan's accident, our family found ourselves at a new level of fucked-upness that can only be scaled at a twelve out of ten. It was December 2021, and as everyone else hung twinkling lights, decorated Christmas trees, baked holiday cookies, watched Christmas movies, and purchased presents for their loved ones, we were taking shifts monitoring the care being provided to Ryan at Einstein Medical Center in Elkins Park. Ryan had been admitted to the medical-surgical floor, recovering from his fourth bout of pneumonia. I was ready to give birth to our son Leo at any point, and the positivity, hope, and vigor for Ryan's care I had possessed while he was in the ICU at Penn Presbyterian was dwindling. In its place was a growing sense of impending doom, exhaustion, and anger. We were beholden to the medical care, or lack thereof, at Einstein Medical Center because Ryan was too weak to endure the intensive therapies at Moss Rehabilitation. We had specifically chosen Moss Rehabilitation as the place we wanted Ryan to be transferred after his discharge from the Neuro ICU at Penn because we were told that was where miracles happened, and it was one of the top ten brain rehabilitation programs in the country. However, there were no miracles happening on the med-surg floor of Einstein Medical Center, only more trauma and setbacks. We were forced to navigate medical care, which was below the standard of care, in a medical facility that just happened to be in the same building where Moss Rehabilitation was nestled because we were told that transferring Ryan to another medical facility could delay his transfer back to the rehabilitation floor. We were in a unique type of hell on earth, and there was no way out but through it.

"Why is my husband's face smashed up against the side of that goddamn hospital bed every time I come in here in the morning?" I shouted at a random nurse who was typing on a computer at the nurse's station outside of Ryan's hospital room. "He can't move himself away from the side of the bed, and you all have him in the most uncomfortable position every time I come in here! It's unacceptable. I want a report from the respiratory therapist about how many times my husband was suctioned last night. There is blood coming from his tracheostomy like they were suctioning him unnecessarily, and now he is all irritated. He only needs to be suctioned if absolutely necessary. Lastly, I want to see my husband's attending physician as soon as possible, and I want to speak to the attending pulmonologist, not just a resident. Okay?" My monologue finally ended with a huff.

"I am not your husband's nurse, ma'am," the poor nurse said, looking at me nervously.

I was on a fucking rampage and could not be stopped at that point. "I don't care who you are; get me someone who can help me. Thank you," I added sarcastically. I stomped back to

Ryan's room, rubbing my pregnant belly from top to bottom because Leo was flipping and making me uncomfortable.

I repositioned Ryan myself by gently pulling his one side away from the hard hospital bed and centering him in the middle of the mattress. "There you go, sweetheart. Much better, right? I'll take care of you. Don't worry, okay?" I said reassuringly as I stroked his forehead and ran my hand through his thick brown hair. I kissed Ryan on the head and then pulled back to look at him. His eyes looked glassy—tired, broken, and sad. It brought me to tears. I wished he could just talk to me for five minutes and let me know what he wanted or if I was doing the right things. I needed him, but he was the only person who couldn't offer me support. Tears rolled down my cheeks thinking about how strong and able Ryan had once been, how he'd always been my protector. Now he needed me to be his. That was a role I could not fail at. I propped pillows on either side of his head to balance it upright, the way that he always looked the most comfortable. Ryan's tracheostomy rattled and crackled from moving him, and he coughed, unearthing lots of green mucus sprinkled with blood onto his hospital gown. I ran to grab some hospital gloves and gauze so I could clean him up properly. I was now a wife, mother, and caretaker to my thirty-five-year-old husband, who'd once been the most lively and capable man. Now he couldn't do anything. My big pregnant belly pushed up against the hospital bed as I leaned over to clean Ryan up, and when I was done, I was out of breath.

I sat in the chair next to Ryan's hospital bed with the lights off and turned on some music, waiting for Ryan's doctors to come in and give me updates. On my phone, I played David Gray's "This

Year's Love," which was our wedding song, and just let the tears go. "You know this song, right, babe?" I said through tears, squeezing his hand tightly three times, which meant "I love you," something Ryan had done to me many times on car rides or whenever else we held hands. I wondered if he knew what I was doing and how much I loved him. I willed him to know how much I cherished him. The song ended, and I hobbled to the bathroom to grab some tissues and clean my face. I looked in the mirror and saw that my mascara had run all the way down my cheeks, past my jawbone, and onto my neck. I turned on the sink, reached over to grab a wad of toilet paper, and ran it under the water. I stared at myself in the mirror and realized I didn't even recognize myself anymore. I had become an entirely different person since Ryan's accident. My instinct to protect him at all costs and make sure he received the best possible care felt like a tsunami—overwhelming and powerful—and I didn't care who it offended or destroyed in its wake. Social norms and graces did not exist in my world anymore, in this world of trauma and sickness. It was survival of the fittest, or more appropriately, survival of a very angry and very pregnant woman who was trying her best to heal her husband at any cost.

I was halfway through cleaning my face when I heard a voice bellowing from Ryan's hospital room, "Hello, Mrs. Allen? Are you here?"

I pushed the door open, the wet wad of toilet paper in my hand and mascara running down half of my face. "Yes, hello, Doctor," I said as I walked over to the side of Ryan's bed near his head.

The doctor had brought the pulmonary resident with him,

and they were standing next to each other, shoulder to shoulder. "I heard you had some questions for me." He sounded annoyed, which pissed me off right away.

"Yes, I have some questions, Doctor. First of all, how many times did my husband get suctioned last night? At Penn, it was explained to us that suctioning Ryan too much would make his secretions worse and irritate him and that the respiratory therapists should wait until his oxygen rate is lowering before suctioning him. From the looks of the blood coming from my husband's tracheostomy, it would appear he was suctioned way more than necessary, and now it is causing more issues," I said angrily.

"I believe he got suctioned four or five times in the night," the doctor said matter-of-factly. I felt a warm sensation move quickly from the pit of my stomach through the top of my throat, and I clenched both my hands in fists. I was furious that Ryan had been suctioned that much throughout the night, knowing how, with each session, his whole body convulsed, shook in pain, and caused an uncontrollable coughing fit. It was also completely unnecessary from what we had learned from the physicians at Penn, and I was very confident in the care that had been provided by Ryan's medical team there. In my gut, I didn't trust anyone at this medical facility, and I didn't feel that Ryan was safe there. I felt like punching both the attending physician and the resident in the face, but thankfully, even in my livid state, I executed some restraint and did not punch them. Instead, I yelled and clapped at the doctors. "HE [clap] DOES [clap] NOT [clap] NEED [clap] TO [clap] BE [clap] SUCTIONED [clap] THAT [clap] FUCKING MUCH [clap]. Do you understand? I want a report from his respiratory therapists every morning to ensure that does not happen again; do you understand?" My hands were shaking.

The attending pulmonologist and the resident stared at me in silence, their eyes wide open in utter disbelief that I had just yelled and clapped at them. "You can't talk to us like that," the attending pulmonologist said as he started to direct the resident out the door.

Although my reaction to Ryan getting unnecessarily suctioned was justified, I knew as the doctors began to walk out the door that I had to play the game, that I had to bury these intense feelings for Ryan's sake and get him well enough that he could get out of this hellscape and back into rehab, where hope still existed. "Listen, I just want what is best for my husband, okay? What can we do to prevent him from being suctioned unnecessarily? Let's come up with a plan here so that it doesn't happen again because it is hurting him, not helping him." That day, the image of an eight-month-pregnant me clapping at two physicians earned me the title of "Gangster Jew" from Karen and Morgan.

* * *

Ryan was days away from dying when I saw a familiar car pull up in front of Michael's house while I was sitting on the massive couch in the formal living room where Ryan was. I felt exhausted and broken, wanting and longing for the end of the nightmare but also dreading the finality of the end with every fiber of my being. I squinted my eyes so I could make out who was about to enter "Happy Hospice," and I saw the familiar bob and sway of the short blonde hair that could only belong to one person—my mother—as she hurriedly approached the front door. "What the fuck is she doing here?" I asked Karen and Morgan. "She didn't even tell me she was coming. If she had given me any sort of warning, I would have told her not to come." Since Ryan's admission to the ICU at Penn Presbyterian, my mother had been pretty much MIA, except for a visit to my home when Leo was first born. Holding a fresh new baby was easy and fun for my mother, but participating in any real and tangible way when her eldest daughter was in and out of hospitals and hospice dealing with a sick and dying husband was, well, not fun or easy.

On the flip side, Ryan's mom, Karen, had taken a leave of absence from work to help me with the boys after Leo was born—sleeping on my sleeper sofa for three months, driving me to my follow-up doctor's appointments, helping me down the stairs when I could barely move after my C-section, bringing me food and water in bed while I nursed Leo, and keeping Jack on schedule and entertained. We navigated going to the hospital to visit Ryan soon after Leo was born, making Ryan's Jeep into a gypsy caravan. Due to COVID restrictions, Karen and Morgan sat in the car with a newborn Leo in the dead of winter while I, still high on Percocet and freshly cut open, could visit Ryan while he was in the long-term acute care hospital Good Shepherd in Bethlehem, Pennsylvania. Karen's selfless acts to help me and our boys embodied what a true mother should be like, and her love was unconditional, with no strings attached. My mother, on the other hand, wanted to make me into a marionette doll, controlling every string of my life and loving me based only on how much control she could exert over me and with a laundry list of conditions. But here she was, showing up like the Messiah again, waiting for everyone to embrace her, as Ryan was so close to death. "What does she expect? A fucking parade? Everyone here has earned the privilege of watching Ryan die. They have shown up through the whole ordeal. It's a fucking privilege to watch someone die. How about you go fuck yourself, Debbie?" I said as I paced back and forth waiting for my mother's voice to bellow in the foyer of Michael's house. Karen and Morgan just stared at me wide-eyed. I paced myself into Michael's kitchen and waited.

"Hello?" Debbie called into the foyer. I couldn't even greet her without wanting to punch her in the face. I knew Ryan would want me to be strong and tell her to take a hike. I waited in the kitchen for a few minutes, getting up the nerve to tell her to leave. I finally took a deep breath and opened the two glass doors that led from Michael's kitchen into his formal living room. There, I found my mother playing obnoxiously loud with Jackson only feet away from Ryan's hospital bed.

"You need to leave, Mother," I said matter-of-factly but confidently.

"Why do I have to leave?" she asked, surprised.

"Mother, you are not wanted here. You think you can just show up whenever you want, and it is inappropriate. Please leave," I repeated.

"But I'm family!"

Ah, yes, the magic words. My mother was a master manipulator at using blood as a reason to treat people like complete shit without putting in the actual work to earn the title of family. "Mother, get out now." She stood up from the couch in a huff and started toward the front door, her short blonde hair swaying back and forth. She was gone as quickly as she had arrived. I noticed my fists were clenched into balls, and when I unclenched them, I realized I was shaking.

Karen shouted, "Gangster Jew!" I looked at her and smiled, relieved. Most importantly, I knew Ryan wouldn't want my mother witnessing his death, and he would have given me a high-five for kicking her out of hospice.

* * *

I entered Ryan's hospital room at Good Shepherd Specialty Care Hospital on January 11, 2022, for the first time in more than three weeks. I opened the door slowly, afraid of what condition Ryan would be in when I first saw him, as he had been on lockdown with no visitors. I had tested positive for COVID two weeks prior, at nine months pregnant, and our family had done the right thing by advising the hospital staff of my positive test. They had immediately put Ryan on a red alert for fourteen days. We reasoned that the risk of Ryan contracting or spreading COVID was far less than the risk of him mentally deteriorating due to lack of stimulation, especially if he tested negative for COVID, which is exactly what happened. His physician at Moss Rehabilitation had also agreed with this sentiment. We had yelled, screamed, and cursed on the phone, begging the hospital and administrative staff at Good Shepherd, including a horrible social worker, to make an exception due to Ryan's fragility from his brain injury. We used every reasonable argument in an attempt to convince the hospital to continue to let healthy family members visit Ryan, promising that each visitor would take a rapid COVID test before each visit to prove their negative status and wear N95 masks, gowns, and gloves—anything so Ryan could continue to get the human interaction he so desperately needed to improve and recover. I had even threatened to sue the hospital if anything happened to him, and I meant it with every cell in my body. Unfortunately, we realized having to navigate caring for a sick family member during the time of COVID was like living within an alternate universe, where weighing the risks and benefits of anything else besides COVID didn't exist. It was a battle we could not win, no matter how hard we fought. So, Ryan's only allotted stimulation for two weeks was two thirty-minute FaceTime calls a week, where we talked into a phone to a man who couldn't even speak back to us.

* * *

I hobbled to Ryan's bedside, high on Percocet and still sore and tender from my C-section only nine days earlier. Leo was a newborn and had already made the hour-long trek to Bethlehem, Pennsylvania, so that I could go visit Ryan. Bundled tightly in a blanket, Leo would lie on Karen's or Morgan's lap in Ryan's Jeep in the hospital parking lot, with the heat blasting, in the dead of winter between my nursing sessions with him. We were hospital gypsies with a newborn baby in tow. It was both hilarious and completely fucked up at the same time.

"Hi, sweetheart. It's me. I'm so sorry it took me so long to come back. I missed you so much." I whispered as I carefully leaned forward to kiss Ryan's forehead while he slept in his hospital bed. The room was eerily quiet and dimly lit with just the long, horizontal fluorescent lights behind Ryan's bed. "We had another baby, boo. Leo is perfect and looks just like you," I said, now through tears. I brushed the back of my hand against Ryan's cheek. "Can you open your eyes for me? I love seeing your beautiful eyes," I asked Ryan eagerly. Prior to Ryan's two-week lockdown, he had been able to respond to minimal commands from me specifically. This time, my request went unanswered by Ryan, who continued to lie completely still in his hospital bed. I suddenly felt a sharp pain in my abdomen from my incision site and decided that if I wanted to make it the entire two hours before having to hobble back to the car to nurse Leo, I should sit down. My Percocet was wearing off quickly. I pulled a cream-colored hospital chair over to Ryan's bedside and lowered myself slowly to avoid any abrupt movements that I knew would cause me to wince in pain. I took Ryan's hand and interlocked our fingers as I analyzed Ryan's face and breathing. He somehow looked different than he had before the lockdown. It was as if the beam of light that I felt had surrounded him prior to his quarantine, like a symbol of hope, had burned out. Ryan's light was gone, and I could sense it. I will never know exactly what happened to Ryan over those two weeks, but I believe that due to the lack of human interaction, he had given up and succumbed to his brain injury. He was so tired of fighting, as we all were. Without us at his side day after day, giving him the motivation to keep fighting and reminding him what he was fighting for, Ryan had stopped trying to come back to us and went permanently into the darkness. Looking at Ryan in that moment, I knew that he would never come home to our family as a whole person. His light had disappeared, and the hope of Ryan's recovery along with it. I put my head on Ryan's leg as I squeezed his hand and sobbed into the white hospital sheet.

* * *

It was the end of February 2022. We had made the final decision to put Ryan on hospice but still had a few weeks to get affairs in order before he was officially discharged from Moss Rehabilitation, scheduled for March 17, and moved to Michael's house, his last stop before heaven. With the knowledge that we were shifting gears from trying to bring Ryan home to allowing Ryan to die and have peace, we began researching venues for his memorial service. One afternoon, I googled "funeral homes in Doylestown," not really knowing what else to search for this particular need, but a location close to home seemed important. Varcoe Thomas Funeral Home popped up with dozens of five-star reviews, which I thought was odd for a funeral home. But I figured if Google reviews could help me find a good sushi restaurant, they could help me find a decent funeral home for my husband. We decided to take a rare afternoon that we were all together and not separated between rehabilitation and other responsibilities to call Varcoe Thomas to get information about what their services would entail. We had decided that Ryan would not want to be buried, tied to a particular physical location forever, but that he would want to be cremated so we could spread his ashes in his favorite places. The cremation option seemed more like Ryan; he would physically be free, unlike the state he was in at the moment. The thought of spreading his ashes in the places he loved the most in this world, including our backyard, gave me some peace.

"Karen, you're gonna have to make this call," I said as we sat at my dining room table. I'd been tasked with making several really difficult phone calls earlier in the week, telling some of Ryan's best friends that we were putting him on hospice, and I was burned out.

"No problem. I can do it," Karen replied as she started to dial the funeral home's number on her cell phone. After so many months of Ryan in the hospital and in rehabilitation and having to manage his medical care, insurance coverage nightmares, logistics with visiting, COVID restrictions, a newborn baby and a toddler, and an endless number of other impossible tasks, we had become a well-oiled trauma machine, delegating when necessary and dividing the duties fairly and according to how much shit each of us could take on one particular day. Fortunately, it always seemed that at least one of us had the fortitude to take on more on any given day. The trauma duties rotated evenly throughout Ryan's ordeal. It was like having a trauma chore wheel, and Karen, Morgan, and I spun the shit out of that thing every single day.

Karen's cell phone rang on speaker as I attempted to clean up my kitchen, and Morgan sat with her computer at the dining room table. "Hello, this is Varcoe Thomas Funeral Home, Madison speaking," a soft voice on the other end of the phone said.

"Hello, Madison. My name is Karen Allen. I am calling because we will be needing your services for my son in the near future, and we wanted to get more information," Karen said hesitantly. I could tell she didn't really know how to explain our situation to a funeral home, considering Ryan was still alive. "Okay, I see. Can you tell me the name of the deceased?"

"Oh, he isn't dead yet," Karen said, holding back a laugh. Karen's comment was funny but also painfully tragic. After so many months of trauma, we had become desensitized to things that should have made us sad or that would have normal, nontraumatized people in tears. Instead, uncomfortable situations like calling a funeral home about what to do with Ryan's body after he was dead had become a fucked-up comedy show. Morgan and I began laughing hysterically at Karen's response to Madison. Neither of us could restrain ourselves, and in turn, Karen started laughing hysterically, too.

Madison, on the other hand, seemed completely unfazed. "Oh, I see," Madison said calmly. Karen got a hold of herself, and Madison started explaining the different viewing services options. Madison was completely immune to our bizarre responses as we continued to laugh uncontrollably on the other end of the phone. Madison continued her death spiel, now beginning to explain the different cremation options to us. "Our basic cremation option costs $1,995," explained Madison.

Morgan piped up like she couldn't help herself, "It sounds like a Walmart special." That was it; we all began laughing uncontrollably again. I laughed so hard I had to steady myself against my marble countertops. Through tears of laughter, I thought to myself how much Ryan would think this entire situation was all so ridiculous and how funny he would have found our completely inappropriate phone interaction with the ever so calm and sweet young woman at Varcoe Thomas Funeral Home as she talked about viewings, cremation, and obituaries. Our laughter was a classic trauma response. We were deep in the trenches, so deep that we had to laugh to keep from crying. Sometimes the absurdity of it all was too much to process. We were laughing because of the irony of it all and because we were exhausted and utterly depleted after five months of hell. Ryan was going to die because of the decision we had made in love as a family to set him free, and that was the very unfunny reality of the situation. Standing over my kitchen sink, I suddenly felt sick to my stomach thinking about Ryan's beautiful body being burned into ash at the affordable price of $1,995.

CHAPTER 9
RAGE LAWNING, XANAX, AND COSMOS

"DO I NEED TO CALL SOMEONE?" I HOLLERED through the open sliding glass door to my mother-in-law, Karen. I had just seen her from the window with an axe, which she had gotten from God knows where, ragefully cutting down low-lying branches from a tree in my backyard. Truth be told, Karen does most chores with rage, including rage cleaning, rage cooking, rage putting on toddler shoes, and rage shutting doors, to name just a few. Ironically, the only thing she doesn't do with rage is pick up dog shit—that she does zenfully. I had never experienced what I now call Karen's rage lawning, but here it was in full force, and I was a little worried.

* * *

Leading up to Karen's rage lawning episode, we had preliminarily decided to put Ryan on hospice after almost six months of hospitalizations and rehabilitation stays with him making no tangible mental progress. It was our secret, something we dared not share with the world until the decision was to be finalized in a few days after speaking with Ryan's team at Moss Rehab. This secret felt heavy and devastating every time people asked me earnestly, "How is Ryan doing? Is he making improvements?" Our hopes continued to be shattered as each day passed, and we saw Ryan deteriorate both mentally and physically. He no longer responded to the few commands he once had, and he looked like an even sicker version of himself, bony and fragile, so unlike the strong man I once knew and adored.

Ryan's copious secretions through his tracheostomy had stabilized, and he had been able to tolerate intensive therapies at Moss, but we still spent most of our time with him cleaning up bodily fluids that had spurted out from the tube and onto his shirt—a harsh reminder that Ryan could no longer take care of himself and was completely dependent on family and medical staff for all activities of daily living. Ryan grimaced with pain when certain limbs were moved because his brain injury had also caused him to develop a condition leading to hyperactive bone growth. His beautiful pink mouth curled when his knees were flexed or bent. It was like a stab to the heart every time I saw him in pain. Ryan's body folded forward like a rag doll every time the therapy staff at Moss transferred him from his hospital bed to his wheelchair and vice versa for his therapies, his long legs dangling and swaying in the Hoyer lift suspended from the ceiling. I found myself hiding in the bathroom during these transfers and for Ryan's diaper changes to avoid having to look at these god-awful scenes anymore. After five months, I could no longer watch the love of my life be more helpless than our almost two-month-old baby boy. Ryan was suffering, and I could see it written all over his face. Leading up to the decision to transition Ryan from rehabilitation care to hospice care, it became clearer and clearer that we were nearing the end of our hope for a miracle and that we had done everything in our power to bring Ryan back. Ryan had even participated in an Ambien trial that was a last Hail Mary to see if he would transition out of the disordered state of consciousness he was in. He had the best doctors, the best rehabilitation, and the best treatment for brain injuries, but it was no use. Ryan was never meant to come back to us, and I kept hearing his voice in my head over and over. *Babe, just let me go. It's time.* And he was right, but my heart ached with the thought of letting him go.

* * *

"I'm *fine*!" Karen hollered back at me from the backyard as she swung the axe back and forth in the crisp air. "This tree really needed its branches taken care of," she said breathlessly as she threw dead branches into a large brown paper bag.

I called Morgan, who was at her house, on FaceTime. I held the camera to the scene of Karen rage lawning as Morgan accepted the FaceTime video. "Morgan! You have to come here. Your mother is losing it, and I'm a little worried." I was laughing so hard I was crying.

"Oh dear . . ." Morgan's voice trailed off. "What the hell is she doing?" Morgan asked.

"I think this is what we would call rage lawning," I explained through my laughter. I remember thinking to myself at that moment how strange life was—how the worst possible thing could be happening in the background, but I could still laugh so hard I cried, and I could still feel joy even though I had no peace at the moment. We had all used laughter as a form of self-preservation since Ryan's accident, and it was these fleeting moments of humor, often dark humor, that kept us sane throughout Ryan's ordeal. "Karen! Do you need me to call your doctor and see if we can get you a prescription for Xanax?" I asked, only half-serious.

"This *is* my medication," she responded in jest but a bit crazily, wiping sweat from her forehead with her wrist since her hands were in Ryan's yard gloves.

"Okay. Well, I am here if you need me!" I yelled as I shut the sliding glass door. I rolled my eyes into the phone at Morgan as if to say, *what in the actual fuck?*

"So that's why you need to come back here, Morgan," I joked, but in reality, I was serious. We were all dealing with the reality of making the final decision to put Ryan on hospice in our own way. I was dealing with the reality by eating lots of sad cake, drinking Blue Moons and vodka seltzers, rage Pelotoning (yes, that's a thing), and cleaning obsessively. Morgan had once caught me during one of my cleaning fits on my hands and knees in my kitchen, scrubbing my baseboards, which were already whiter than white. I said goodbye to Morgan and stood silently in the playroom, staring at the picture of Ryan on my phone's lock screen. He was smiling his movie-star smile, and he was kneeling on the ground, with Louie sitting next to him. He looked so content, proud, and strong. I snapped back to the present moment and thought again about the fact that in a few short days, we would be announcing to the world that we were putting Ryan on hospice, that we were done fighting, and so was

Ryan. A familiar wave of nausea washed over me as I began to make my way to Leo's nursery to wake him up from a nap.

* * *

It was early in the morning, and I stumbled downstairs with Leo in my arms, no bra on and breast milk soaking through the T-shirt I had slept in. It was the first week of April 2022, nine days since stopping Ryan's feeds and any hydration while on hospice, and he was still here living and breathing, but barely. "He looks like a fucking skeleton," I said to myself as I walked past Morgan. I looked over at Ryan, my sweet boy, whose bones were now jutting out of his skin. His collarbones looked as if they could pierce his skin at any moment, and his cheekbones stuck out prominently from his sunken cheeks. His eyes looked dark and hollow, like he was already dead, despite the small movements of his chest slowly rising and falling. Ryan's skin on his feet and legs had started to develop a marbled purple color, called mottling, which was spreading rapidly up his body. I already knew what this meant—that his body was no longer able to pump blood effectively and that Ryan's death was imminent. The blood was moving away from his extremities and to his vital organs to try to keep him alive.

"I need fucking coffee," I said, exasperated. I had been up for less than five minutes, and I was already disgusted with the day. "Want to hold a cute baby?" I asked Morgan as I held baby Leo under his armpits facing out in her direction.

Morgan was sitting cross-legged on Michael's plush sofa, reading a book. "Come here, baby!" Morgan reached out her arms enthusiastically to take Leo, our little shining star in the darkness, from me so I could pour myself some coffee in the kitchen. Ryan was dying, and soon. I figured caffeine would make me feel less like I wanted to join him. I poured my coffee in the kitchen and then made my way to the leather chair across from Ryan's hospital bed. I nestled my legs up on the side of the chair like a mermaid, placed my elbow on my thigh and the palm of my hand on the side of my face, and stared at Ryan in complete horror.

"What other drugs can he have?" I pleaded with Ryan's nurse desperately, who was just a few feet away in the living room.

"I will have to check his chart. I'm pretty sure he is getting everything he can get right now. Maybe I can give him more Ativan and add some Haldol," Ryan's nurse told me calmly.

I stared at her blankly for a moment before responding. "Just give him whatever you fucking can. Load him the fuck up. I don't care what you have to do. This is ridiculous. Look at him, for Christ's sake! He is a skeleton! How is he still here?" I felt the familiar lump in my throat developing and tears welling up in my eyes. This was too much to ask of someone—to have to watch the beautiful, witty, brave, and caring man I was in love with die in this barbaric, drawn-out way right in front of my eyes. And I couldn't save him. No one could save him. I felt hopeless, powerless, and weak. I didn't think I could experience one more second of this excruciating agony. My whole body felt like it was about to explode into a million pieces. But I just sat there chugging my coffee, staring at a skeleton that was once my husband. I needed this to be over. Ryan's family needed this to be over. Most importantly, Ryan needed this to be over.

Ryan's nurse looked at me and nodded her head as if she was reading my mind. Her eyes looked glassy with tears as she turned around to walk into the kitchen to get the additional medication I had demanded to help Ryan die.

* * *

"What is that red stuff in Ryan's urinal bag? Is that blood?" Karen worriedly asked the room. My eyes darted to the urinal bag that was hanging from Ryan's hospital bed, which we had all been staring at and analyzing for the past nine days since we had stopped Ryan's feedings and hydration. "Is that blood?" Karen asked again, and this time her own question prompted her to start sobbing uncontrollably. Morgan and I looked at each other from across the room with that familiar what-the-fuck look written all over our faces—a habitual look we gave each other during Happy Hospice.

"It's just too much," Morgan said as she got up from the couch and walked into the kitchen. Ryan was so dehydrated by this time that there were no extra fluids in his body to expel, so he was bleeding into his urinal bag, a sign his body was shutting down. In the six months since Ryan's accident, I had been up close and personal to bags full of Ryan's feces, urine, and sputum with no issues, often eating full meals within inches without batting an eye, but seeing blood in his urinal bag as he lay actively dying next to me sent shivers up my spine. I put my head down, placed my palm on my forehead, shut my eyes, and just shook my head back and forth as I listened to Karen's sobbing. Her cries were excruciating, the type of cries that only a mother could cry for her dying child. It was unbearable. I could feel her pain with each wail and howl as I got up from my seat and followed Morgan into the kitchen.

"What should we do about your mom?" I asked Morgan. "She isn't doing well."

"I don't know," Morgan said, taking a deep sigh.

None of us were holding up very well, but especially not Karen. Her wails continued in the other room as she repeated over and over, "My beautiful boy. Oh, my beautiful boy . . ."

* * *

A small, walnut-colored box caught my eye as I was washing my hands in Michael's kitchen sink. The sunlight forced its rays through the big window facing me and hit the side of my face. I dried my hands, picked up the box, and read the word "Happiness," which was carved delicately on the top. I slid the top of the box open and noticed several small white pills inside, one of which was cut in half, the jagged edges of the pill noticeable. I walked back into the living room, where everyone was now gathered and talking. The overall tone of the room had calmed since the morning's terrible happenings, and Karen was sitting on one side of the couch with an almost empty cup in her hand.

"What are you drinking, Karen?" I asked.

"Umm . . . I'm chasing half a Xanax with a leftover cosmopolitan that Lynn made." She smiled and giggled to herself.

"Okay . . . wow, look at you. All Xanaxed up, I see. Well, it is the early afternoon. Good for you." I laughed at the sight of a drugged-up Karen, who just a couple of hours before had been uncontrollably sobbing at Ryan's deathbed. This was a much more pleasant and bearable sight. I stood and stared at Karen with a smile on my face as she looked straight ahead with a grin on her face, all fucked up.

Right then, Ryan's uncle Gary and Aunt Joan walked in the door and into the living room. "Oh hey, Gil!" Karen said excitedly at first, but then her voice trailed off like she had forgotten something. We all started laughing hysterically since there was no one named Gil in the room. Karen was so relaxed on Xanax and leftover cosmo that she wasn't even able to pronounce her brother's name. "Gil" was the only thing she could force out of her mouth between slurred speech. I laughed so hard I cried, and I felt a temporary wave of relief from the sadness and anxiety I had been feeling all day. I knew it was only temporary, but at that moment, I pretended my biggest worry was that my mother-in-law had just taken half a Xanax and downed a cosmopolitan before 2:00 p.m.

* * *

It was a few days after Ryan had been admitted to the Neuro ICU of Penn Presbyterian Medical Center following his accident. I was sitting in a complete daze next to his hospital bed on the fifth floor. I was completely exhausted due to little to no sleep but wired from adrenaline and the massive amounts of caffeine and sugar from the baked goods I was surviving on. Ryan was in a coma, being kept alive by a ventilator and an army of medications that were automatically being administered by several pumps fashioned on both sides of his hospital bed. He had a medical device in his head that was measuring the pressure in his brain in real time. The "bolt," as it was called, was white and stuck straight up in the air. It was kept in place with white medical tape against a portion of Ryan's head that had to be shaved. I remember looking at Ryan in his hospital bed and thinking that even with all the tubes down his throat, he still looked like Ryan, the handsome man I had loved for almost ten years. It pained me that he looked as if he could just wake up at any moment but that he was just too sick to do so. In my complete and utter daze, I barely noticed when one of the physician assistants on Ryan's medical team came into Ryan's hospital room and started talking to me. It caught me by surprise that this conversation was not just about what the medical team was doing to help Ryan in the moment. Instead, he was telling me more about Ryan's prognosis, given all the clinical information they knew at the time. I found myself completely caught off guard by the conversation, so I just stared and listened as well as I could in my sleep-deprived, adrenaline-induced stupor.

"He will never be the same again," the physician assistant said plainly as if he was ordering a coffee or breakfast sandwich. And there it was. The statement I had not wanted to hear from anyone and had refused to believe when newly entrenched in Ryan's recovery journey. I knew how bad Ryan's condition was, but I still hoped for a miracle and truly believed at that time that a miracle would happen. How could a miracle not happen? My life had always been so charmed. *Something this tragic couldn't possibly happen to our family*, I thought as I stared at the physician assistant as he said those words again since I looked like I wasn't registering anything at that moment. "He will never be the same." I nodded my head and turned my twenty-seven-weeks-pregnant body toward Ryan in his hospital bed and squeezed his hand. I didn't want any more details about what the PA meant. I couldn't handle it at the moment. He sensed my complete lack of readiness for this type of conversation and slowly walked out of the room. I watched him turn the corner, and I was suddenly overwhelmed by panic as his simple statement brought every ounce of hope for a miracle to a screeching halt. The vision of my life with Ryan and our two boys crashed down into a huge pile of rubble, completely unrecognizable from my life before October 14, 2021.

I started crying, and in between tears, I could feel my breathing getting more and more rapid and shallow until I was in a full-blown panic attack. Sweat dripped down my forehead, beads emerged on my chest and the back of my neck, and I started losing sensation in my lips and the tips of my fingers. I felt myself tunneling into a black hole, close to passing out, when Ryan's nurse ran in, having seen me from the hallway. "Can I get some ice packs in here?" she yelled loudly into the hallway. "It's okay, it's okay. You need to calm down; you're pregnant. Deep breaths, deep breaths, deep breaths," she said calmly as she lifted my hair from the back of my neck and fanned my neck and face. "This isn't over. They don't really know what is going to happen. Let's just focus on the here and now, okay? Deep breaths." Her reassuring and kind voice brought me back to my body and into the light as my breathing regulated. In my mind, I knew a meaningful recovery from Ryan's severe brain injury was unlikely. But in my heart, I still hoped for a miracle.

CHAPTER 10

OUR DOUBLE RAINBOW

IT WAS JUST AFTER 6:00 A.M. ON MAY 16, 2022, when I found myself racing down Edison Furlong Road in my BMW. I was trying to get to Doylestown Hospital as fast as I could. I had just learned that Steve Plum Jr., Ryan's best friend and my dear friend, was dead. He had suffered a sudden cardiac arrest in his home in front of his wife, Nancy, and their four children. Ryan had died just five weeks earlier, and it had only been two weeks since Ryan's memorial service, where Steve had shared a funny and heartfelt eulogy. Nancy, a veteran nurse, had tried to save Steve, just like I had tried to save Ryan, but unlike Ryan, Steve could not be revived. I knew Steve had been in cardiac arrest for a long time, and I was relieved for Nancy and her children that if Steve had to die, if it was his time, she didn't have to go through the hell of caring for a spouse with a brain injury. This was a truth many people would not understand, but one I knew intimately. I had left my home in total disbelief and shock, barely able to forge a coherent thought or sentence. All I could manage to say to our nanny was, "I have to go!" Jackson asked what was wrong as I was frantically trying to put on a bra and pants so I could leave for the hospital. All I could think as I stared at him was, *fuck, fuck, fuck!*

* * *

I was one left turn away from Doylestown Hospital, and the light was red. I looked both ways to make sure no cars were coming and pushed on the gas as hard as I could. I didn't know what I was going to do when I got to the hospital, but I knew I couldn't get to my friend fast enough. Traffic laws be damned. After finally parking, I ran through the same emergency room doors I had entered seven months prior when I didn't know if Ryan was dead. Now I knew that on the other side of those doors was a dead Steve and my beautiful friend Nancy who had just lost her husband, best friend, soulmate, and the father of her four children. My heart ached for her, knowing exactly what that felt like, as the automatic doors of the emergency room opened around me, and I sped past the security guard. "I need to see Nancy Plum. She is back there with her husband, Steve. I need to see them," I demanded to the elderly man sitting on a high stool in the vestibule.

"Ma'am, please calm down. First off, you need to wear a mask. And second of all, are you family? Only family is allowed back."

"I *am* family," I barked at him as I grabbed one of the surgical masks out of the cardboard box he was carrying around. And I meant it. Steve and Nancy were my family, although they were not my blood, and I didn't feel like I was lying when I said that. "We have established that I'm family, and I have a mask now; can you please take me back?" I had no patience anymore. I must have said this very convincingly because the security guard started to lead me to where the trauma bays were—the same trauma bays where they'd taken Ryan after his accident. I pushed aside the curtain and found myself in the same trauma bay where a hospitalist had told me that Ryan's prognosis was "poor," where I stared at my husband on a hospital bed, barely alive, before he was airlifted to Penn Presbyterian.

The room was dark. As I entered, Nancy immediately turned her head to see who had come in. I ran to her with open arms. "Oh my God, Nancy. I am so sorry." There were no other words. I embraced her as hard as I could and let her sob into my shoulder.

"He was my best friend," she cried.

"I know, sweetheart, I know, I know," I whispered as I stroked the back of her head. I held her for a long while, willing her pain away, willing for this not to be reality, willing for Steve to be alive so my dear friend wouldn't have to navigate life without her partner and so that more precious children wouldn't have to grow up without their amazing father. I, personally, had already been through the worst days of my life and survived. I was in a different place than when Ryan's accident happened, and I felt like I could take on Nancy's pain; I wished it so. And there was strength in that. A strength I so wanted to give my friend while I held her, knowing how devastated, hopeless, and defeated she felt.

Nancy and I finally ended our embrace, and my attention turned to Steve's body lying peacefully on the hospital bed in the middle of the room. This was the second dead body I had seen in six weeks. First my husband, and now his best friend. But I didn't feel that familiar lump in my throat that was followed by inevitable tears. Instead, I felt numb looking at Steve's lifeless body, which was also accompanied by a strange sense of peace. If it was Steve's time to go, Ryan had his best friend with him in heaven. As I looked at Steve, I thought of Ryan greeting Steve with a huge smile and a hug, saying, "What's up, man? What took you so long?" It was a beautifully sad image. I walked over to Steve, put my hand on his forearm, and squeezed it. "Hey, bud," I whispered to Steve. "Say hi to Ryan for me, okay? I love you. Thank you for everything."

* * *

Karen and Morgan joined me at the hospital to support Nancy and her family. We waited outside the hospital until Steve's body was taken to the coroner, followed by a police escort. The images of all the flashing police cars and the sounds of multiple K9s barking and police and ambulance sirens brought me back to what is still the worst day of my life—the day I lost Ryan to an insidious brain injury. It was the last day I heard Ryan's laugh, saw his smile. The last day he was able to give me a kiss or give Jackson a hug. A chill went down my spine as I began to embody some of the emotions from that day. The fear and anxiety of the unknown and the bottomless pit of sadness in knowing that my life would never be the same.

I looked at Karen and Morgan as the procession came to an end and asked, "So, who needs a drink?" We found ourselves at a corner table by the window of one of my favorite restaurants in Doylestown, called the Hattery, where we could see the main street in town. It was just after 10:30 a.m., and I decided that vodka was the only drink that could touch this day. "Can I please have a vodka soda?" I asked the waitress. Morgan and Karen ordered Bloody Marys. I chugged my first vodka soda and took big bites of the deviled eggs appetizer I'd ordered.

"What in the actual fuck?" Karen said in between sips of her Bloody Mary.

"I just have no words," Morgan said. We sat and drank and ate, stared at each other, and shook our heads in disbelief. I stared at the window, finally feeling a little buzzed but still numb.

"Can I take that?" the waitress asked me, pointing to the glass where the ice from my first vodka drink was melting.

"I'll keep that," I said as I lifted the glass and proceeded to knock back the ice, getting every sip of alcohol I could. Morgan and Karen laughed. It didn't occur to me how bizarre I must have looked. But I didn't care. Ryan was dead, and now Steve was dead, and there was no amount of vodka in the world that could change that.

* * *

I had finally gotten home after spending the day at Nancy's house. I was emotionally drained. I recounted the day's happenings to Karen, who had been watching the boys for me while I was at Nancy's. I heard the familiar chime of my cell phone on the kitchen counter and went to see who had messaged me. It was Nancy, and the message was a picture of a double rainbow. One was a clearer, more vibrant rainbow, and right behind it was a faded, newer-looking rainbow. They were perfectly placed in the sky and could be seen from Nancy's window above Steve's K9 vehicle. "It's our boys," she wrote.

"It's them," I responded. In my heart, I knew Ryan, the more established angel, and Steve, the newer angel, had found each other in heaven and wanted to let Nancy and me know they were happy and at peace.

* * *

I opened the front door and felt a rush of cold winter air hit my face and feet, the only parts of my body that weren't covered by layers of clothing. In front of me was my dear friend Steve Plum Jr. and his one-year-old little girl, Francesca. They were both bundled up in sweatshirts and puffy jackets with big smiles on their faces. "Hey, Whit!" Steve shouted as he gave me a big bear hug, the only kind of hug he knew how to give. Steve had volunteered to come to my home at 7:00 a.m. on a freezing Saturday to pick up Jackson and entertain him and Steve's four children for an entire day by himself while I spent the day at the hospital visiting Ryan. Steve was the kind of friend who showed up even when things were inconvenient and the kind of person who would change his entire schedule if you needed him. He was selfless, generous, kind, and hilarious. The kind of friend who rarely comes along in a lifetime, and I got to reap the benefits of Steve and Nancy's friendship since Steve and Ryan had forged quite the bromance during K9 training, where they'd met. Ryan, Jackson, and I spent many evenings at the Plums' home, eating, laughing, and telling stories. In a few short years, they had become two of our best friends. After Ryan's accident, Steve and Nancy took Jackson for an entire week, drove him to day care, picked him up, fed him, dressed him, bathed him, and loved on him while I was living downtown during a very critical period while Ryan was in the Neuro ICU at Penn Presbyterian. Steve and Nancy hadn't hesitated to take on such a responsibility. It was in their nature to care for their people in such an integral and powerful way. Caring for Jackson as if he was one of their own so I could focus on Ryan's care was a selfless act of kindness I will never forget.

"We are going to have so much fun today, Jack! Are you excited to see some four-wheelers?" Steve said excitedly to Jackson, who was hanging on my leg and still rubbing his eyes from being asleep ten minutes earlier. Jackson's face suddenly lit up when Steve talked to him, and it warmed my heart to know that Jackson would get some time with a male figure for the day, something that had been missing in his life since Ryan's accident. I was so grateful to Steve for loving my little boy so much, for loving our family so much, and I knew how grateful Ryan would be for such a loyal and true friend. "Give Ryan a big hug for me, okay? We are going to have a fun day, and you can just focus on whatever you need to do. I'll drop Jack off later tonight," Steve said with another big smile.

"Thank you so much, Steve. I really appreciate it," I said as Steve turned with Francesca in one arm and Jackson holding his other hand. And I did appreciate it with all my heart, more than I was ever able to express to Steve before he died.

CHAPTER 11

THE TIME CAPSULE

I FOUND MYSELF PARKED IN FRONT OF MY HOUSE for the first time in a week. During the days immediately following Ryan's accident, I had been living downtown to be closer to him in the ICU. Now, I was back where it all started. It was already dark outside, and my headlights illuminated the white garage door. I felt sick in the pit of my stomach as I turned the car's engine off. I was finally home, but Ryan was still fighting for his life in a hospital an hour away. But after a week away from Jackson, I felt he needed his mama and some stability after being shuffled around by friends and family with no routine. My heart and soul were torn apart—longing to be in two different places at once. I opened my car door and felt a rush of cool autumn air hit my face. I helped Jackson out of his car seat and threw several bags full of brand-new clothing people had purchased for me in order to survive a week away from home over my shoulder. Jackson and I walked hand in hand to the front door, and I noticed pieces of plastic in the corners of the front porch from medical equipment the EMS had used on Ryan only days prior. I shivered thinking about those traumatic moments, as they had been replaying over and over in my head nonstop for the last week. The image of Ryan slumped over on our front step, passed out and struggling to breathe, and how his legs and feet had jolted from being shocked flashed in my mind as I inserted the key and slowly turned the lock to open the front door. It was eerily quiet as we entered the house, and the air felt thick and heavy. I walked slowly through our front corridor, still hand in hand with Jackson, and into the kitchen, where I bent over to one side and let all the bags I was holding fall to the floor with a loud thump. I shook out my arms and rubbed my pregnant belly. I was completely and utterly wired from all the adrenaline that had been coursing through my veins for a week straight, keeping me laser-focused and giving me the ability to function. My body, on the other hand, was another story; I was twenty-seven weeks pregnant and living in a hospital, so my body ached all over.

I looked around the kitchen. It was as if nothing had changed since the afternoon of October 14. But in reality, everything had changed. The children's Benadryl I'd had in my hand when I was searching for Ryan and on the phone with EMS on the day of his accident was sitting next to our Nespresso machine. Ryan's Jeep keys and sunglasses were in the middle of the white marble kitchen counter, where he'd tossed them after he had gotten home from the gym right before his accident.

I quickly took Jackson upstairs to put him to bed so I could try to get some sleep too. I had to wake up at 6:00 a.m. to be at Penn Presbyterian in time for the start of visiting hours and rounds with Ryan's physicians. During the rounds, I'd sit in a circle with Ryan's medical team as they gave updates. With a large iced coffee and breakfast sandwich in hand, I'd ask questions, take notes, and deliberately insert myself into being an integral part of his care and treatment. As a medical malpractice defense attorney, I felt at home with the use of complex medical phrases and wasn't afraid of those conversations. Being a part of Ryan's medical rounds made me feel some sense of control, when in reality, I had none.

I clicked on the light upstairs and noticed that Ryan's gym shoes were in the middle of the hallway, exactly where he had taken them off a week prior. I stopped in my bedroom so I could change into pajama pants before putting Jackson to bed and noticed Ryan's laundry basket in our closet. His T-shirts, shorts, boxers, and work pants were piled high in the basket, and I stared at it for a moment. I thought about how everything in the house was unchanged, but my life had been forever and indelibly changed beyond recognition. It felt like I was living in a time capsule—a shrine of my former life prior to Ryan's accident. I felt nauseous thinking of how all the dreams Ryan and I had for our family's future were quickly slipping away. I snapped back to reality after hearing Jackson's sweet voice ask me if we were going to his room so he could go to sleep. He was tired, and so was I. I turned away from Ryan's laundry basket and walked to the door of my bedroom and back into the hallway, where Ryan's gym shoes still lay untouched. It took me months after Ryan's accident to finally wash his laundry. In a strange way, the dirty laundry was my connection to my life prior to October 14, my life with Ryan that I cherished so much. It was something tangible that represented what could have been—what *should* have been. Washing Ryan's laundry felt like a final act, an act that solidified in my own heart and mind that my life would never be the same.

* * *

I sat across from a casually dressed but dashingly handsome Ryan at a small table on the outside patio of the Penn Taproom restaurant in the heart of Doylestown. It was October 12, 2021, two days before Ryan's accident. We were celebrating our eight-year wedding anniversary. We had come directly from a twenty-six-week ultrasound of baby Leo at Doylestown Hospital. Before that, we'd spent the morning in bed watching a movie together, drinking coffee, and eating breakfast sandwiches from Starbucks. We were not only celebrating our wedding anniversary but also the fact that the ultrasound confirmed that Leo was progressing perfectly. The hell of not knowing if he was healthy or not was finally put to rest. Ryan enjoyed a couple of beers and a burger, and I enjoyed a pregnancy-friendly iced tea and salad with grilled salmon on top. It was a perfect October day. I remember how bright the sun was shining and the way the mild breeze blew around the fallen leaves as we talked about Jackson, Ryan's work, and our plans for Leo's nursery. It wasn't an exciting afternoon or anything out of the ordinary. I even recall Ryan saying something about just how boring our lives were and me sweetly reminding him that we were lucky to live such boring lives and that he should try to enjoy each moment, even the mundane and routine ones. Our time together was comfortable, familiar, loving, and intimate. The way we knew what the other was thinking, the way Ryan knew exactly what I would order off the menu and how I would order it, the way he put his hand over mine as we sat in silence, just enjoying each other's company, was the type of experience that can only be shared between two individuals who had spent ten years in a loving relationship and eight years as a happily married couple. I felt grateful and so content as I sat with my hand over my pregnant belly. I watched as Ryan texted someone about work. I sat on the patio of the Penn Taproom that sunny afternoon, so blissfully unaware of how drastically my life would forever change in just forty-eight hours.

CHAPTER 12

LIFE IS A BEAUTIFUL THING

I SAT IN A BRIGHT RED LAWN CHAIR UNDER the awning of Rita's Water Ice and watched as Jackson and Ryan stood in line to order our favorite treats. It was September 2021, still technically summer, but you could feel the subtle change in the atmosphere and weather signaling fall's approach. I could hear the crinkling of fallen leaves scattering across the black asphalt parking lot, and I felt a sudden wave of excitement that the seasons would be changing soon. As I sat and looked at my handsome husband and beautiful son, I felt happy, content, and grateful. I was well into my second trimester of pregnancy with Leo, and we had recently learned he was healthy after being told in July there was a high chance he would have a serious genetic disorder. After undergoing a CVS, a fetal echo, several ultrasounds, and waiting more than two months for all the test results to come back, we were told the preliminary genetic testing had been proven wrong, and we were having a perfect baby boy. I had been in a daze of grief all summer waiting for those test results to come back and was certain they would confirm what our genetic counselor had warned us—that the second baby we so desperately wanted was sick or would die. But then a miracle happened. One test result after the next came back normal, and I sighed a little breath of relief after hearing each one. Little did I know that this trial would be preparing me for the most difficult period of my life in only a few weeks.

"Hey, Jack, who do you want to sit next to? Me or Dadda?" I asked as they returned from the ice cream counter. I already knew the answer, but I asked anyway. I always loved hearing how much Jackson adored Ryan; it warmed my heart and filled me with such joy every time. "Dadda!" he said enthusiastically like he always did. "Of course he wants to sit next to Dadda!" Ryan said as he scooped Jack up under one of his big strong arms while carrying the ice cream treats in the other. We sat and happily ate our ice cream and water ice. I stared at my two beautiful boys in the red lawn chairs next to me, a smile on my face, and moved my hand over my stomach, feeling our other beautiful boy kick and squirm around in my belly. *How did I get so damn lucky?* I asked myself. It was one of the first moments of real peace I had felt in months, and I wished time would stand still for just a little longer so I could bottle up this simple, beautiful memory forever.

* * *

It was April 7, 2022, Ryan's twenty-second day on hospice. It was also his sister Morgan's thirty-third birthday. That day was particularly chaotic, with several people visiting Happy Hospice. Michael's house was loud with talking, laughing, and banter. The mottling on Ryan's skin had moved up from his feet and was now covering his entire body up through his forehead. Ryan was being administered Ativan every half hour to prevent any unnecessary issues with his secretions through his tracheostomy or any myoclonus, shaking spells he had been experiencing since suffering from his brain injury. He was as still as I had seen him on hospice, and he finally looked peaceful. It had been twenty-two days of agony on hospice. Holding the love of my life's hand when I knew he would be dying on that day was a pain I cannot describe. I had been anxious for this time to come, but now that it was here, I didn't want to let him go. I hovered over Ryan's hospital bed and studied his face as I gently stroked the side of his head with the back of my hand. I noticed the curve of his nose and how his lips were the most perfect heart shape at the top, identical to Leo's. His hair was still a rich brown color and thick even after six months of hospitalizations. I ran my hand through it, scratching his scalp like how I used to when we cuddled on the couch watching our favorite shows together. I moved my hand into his and held it, looking at each finger interlocked with my own. Ryan had the most beautiful hands. I felt guilty thinking that I might forget what his hands looked like after he was gone. Morgan came up to me at Ryan's bedside with tears in her eyes. She knew as well as I did that we were finally at the end. And then I broke. "I'm so sorry. I'm so sorry I couldn't save him," I sobbed into Morgan's long blonde hair. I hugged her so tight that I thought she might break, but she embraced me just as hard as if we were trying to keep each other from collapsing.

"It's not your fault. I'm so sorry," she sobbed. We cried and held each other for a long while next to Ryan and then finally released our embrace.

I put my hands on her shoulders and looked at her. "I love you so much, Morgan," I said as confidently as I had ever said anything in my life. Morgan was not my blood, but she was my sister, the true definition of family. I felt so grateful in that moment that she was there and that we could go through this together.

"I love you too," she replied as we embraced again, and more tears soaked our cheeks.

* * *

"It's time. He is going," the head hospice nurse, Tracy, said frantically as she ran over to me. She didn't want me to miss Ryan dying, and she knew how important it was for us to experience his last moments. The room was so loud, with everyone talking, that no one heard her except for me, and I immediately ran over to Ryan's bedside. It was so like Ryan to not want to be the center of attention even when he was freaking dying. Looking back, I feel like Ryan had designed his last moments so perfectly to protect us. He wanted us to be distracted in the moments leading up to his last breaths because he knew how devastated, heartbroken, and defeated we'd feel. He wanted to make his true final moments as easy as possible for the people he loved the most in the world. Making the decision to let Ryan die with dignity was our ultimate and last gift to him, but this was his last gift to us. Even moments before death, Ryan knew how to be selfless, and he was my hero for it. I felt a wave of gratitude in the ocean of sadness and despair I was drowning in that I'd had the honor of being his person for ten years, his wife for eight of those years, and that I'd had the privilege of taking care of him the six months prior to his death. I sat next to my living, breathing, beautiful husband one more time. I put one hand on his chest and held his hand in my other. Ryan's breathing was shallow, and the mottling in his face was extremely prominent on his cheeks and forehead. His skin looked waxy and clammy as he struggled to take in air. As I sat next to Ryan's hospital bed, Karen, Morgan, and John rushed over after Tracy told them what was going on. Like the afternoon of his accident, I could only focus on Ryan. I have no real recollection of what happened around me during the moments directly prior to Ryan's death. I watched him intently as he continued to take shallow breaths. His last, final breath was fuller and lively. It caught me off guard as he inhaled one last time and then curled his lips up in a smile—a smile I had not seen in months—and then, he fell completely still. Ryan was gone. The hell was over.

"Did you see that? He smiled! I've never seen that before. He *smiled*!" Tracy seemed amazed, but I wasn't. It was Ryan, and Ryan was special. His final act in between life and death had been to smile—because he was finally free.

* * *

I found myself staring at Ryan's dead body in the hospice bed that he had been slowly deteriorating in for twenty-two days. I had watched him in bed for countless hours over six months, analyzing his every breath and movement. Complete and utter stillness now replaced the rhythmic rising and falling of Ryan's chest I had meticulously studied over that time. Ryan's face, neck, and body were no longer painted the death-colored purple mottling they had been prior to him dying. I remember thinking how surprisingly normal his coloring looked in the moments following his death. Someone made a comment about how good Ryan's coloring looked, and the nurse explained it was because he was no longer struggling or fighting. I remember thinking how much sense that made to me. I suddenly noticed that everyone who had been in Michael's house at the time of Ryan's last breath was surrounding his bed in a big circle. They were hugging and crying. But it was the first time in many days that I didn't feel like crying. In fact, I felt a lightness I hadn't felt in six months. I knew exactly what I needed to do next, and that was to get the hell out of that house and go home with my babies. I knew Ryan wouldn't want me to linger in the place he had died. He would want me to take our babies home to an environment that meant stability, safety, and comfort to them—to the home we had built together.

I lingered at the top of Ryan's bed near his head, stroked his forehead with the back of my hand, and then ran my hands through his hair. I pictured Ryan somewhere calm and beautiful near the ocean, in a simple white T-shirt and jeans. He was running barefoot on the sand, smiling and laughing. He was finally whole again, and I was so happy for him. The peaceful image of Ryan free and unencumbered by his sick brain kept replaying in my mind as I pushed my way through all the people surrounding Ryan's bed. I went upstairs to pack up our things as we waited for Ryan's body to get picked up and transported to the funeral home, where he would be cremated. It was time to go home. My sister, Rachel, followed me upstairs to help me pack. She understood exactly how I felt. She knew why I wasn't crying; she knew how exhausted I was, how ready I was to go home and start living my life again with my boys, how I was completely over the unknown and the waiting, and how the day that Ryan died was not the worst day I'd had to endure since Ryan's accident. There was no more suffering and no more trying to predict what would happen next. There was a definiteness in Ryan's death that was comforting. As I folded clothes and placed them carefully in bags, I heard the front door open several times, and more voices started slowly filling the downstairs. My husband was dead, and I didn't feel any kind of rush or obligation to make my appearance downstairs as the newly anointed young widow.

I finally made my way down the stairs of Michael's house with my arms full of a plethora of different bags I had endearingly named my "gypsy bags." Officers from Ryan's department had made their way over to Michael's house to see Ryan off with a police escort to the funeral home. Ryan's K9, Louie, was also roaming around the house with his new handler. It was chaotic and noisy, and I just wanted to get the fuck out of there, but I had to wait until they took Ryan's body away. I gently smiled, nodded, and thanked people as they hugged me and offered their condolences. Each one tilted their heads as they looked at me with pity like I was a broken doll whose pieces would never be able to be put together again. As sweet and genuine as everyone's gestures were, I felt annoyed and angry. I didn't need or want their pity, and I knew the last thing Ryan would want for me was to openly accept people's pity for our family's situation. Ryan always hated when people played the victim. In that moment, as my husband lay dead in the next room, I made the decision to never make myself a victim.

In a bit of a sleep-deprived daze, I made my way to the room where Ryan was, sat in one of the large dark-brown leather chairs, and waited for them to take him away. A large gray van pulled up to the house shortly thereafter. I looked out the window as a young man pulled a gurney out of the trunk. He methodically opened the gurney and wheeled it to the front door. They wheeled the gurney into Michael's living room, forcing people to part to let it pass. I stared at the velvet body bag that would shortly envelop Ryan like a mummy, and I felt numb. Several of Ryan's closest family and friends lifted Ryan's body from his hospital bed to the gurney that would wheel him away for the last time. I watched intently as they positioned his body perfectly in the center of the gurney and in the middle of the green velvet body bag. They zippered the bag slowly, the chunky gold zipper moving up Ryan's body as it covered him. His body disappeared into the green fabric, part by part, until it went over his face, and I could no longer see my beautiful boy.

Logically, I knew it was impossible for Ryan to be cold or need comforting, but logic meant little at a time like that. I wanted him to have something comfortable and familiar with him. At my request, they also covered Ryan with a blanket that had traveled with him from the ICU to Moss Rehab, to the specialty care hospital in Bethlehem, back to Moss Rehab, to hospice, and now to his ultimate destination. The blanket was white, black, blue, and gray and had a picture of a K9 on it. It was one of the first gifts we had received after Ryan's accident. It was special, and I wanted him to have it until the very end. They then began to wheel Ryan out of the house to the van outside. I watched as the wheels of the gurney bumped over the uneven parts of the walkway as it made its way to the street. It had been raining heavily at the time of Ryan's death, but when Ryan was wheeled away, it was only misty and cloudy outside. The young man collapsed the gurney's legs, a few men hoisted the gurney up, and Ryan disappeared into the back of the van. A few minutes later, the van pulled away and was closely followed by several Hatboro police vehicles, one of which was playing Ryan's favorite song on its loudspeaker, "Santeria" by Sublime. I watched the van from the open front door as it slowly made its way down Michael's quiet street, the sound of "Santeria" slowly drifting away into the mist, until I could no longer see it. I took a deep breath and stared out the front door for another moment. I then turned and walked to where my bags were piled on the floor in front of the staircase and started to load the bags into my arms to take them to my car and go home.

* * *

I had never been in a funeral home before. But at the age of thirty-five, I found myself at Varcoe Thomas Funeral Home in Doylestown to say my last goodbyes to my husband's body before he was cremated. Our three-month-old and four-year-old were at home with the nanny. The funeral director, Mr. Oz, had asked me if I wanted some time alone with Ryan before the rest of the family said their goodbyes. I said yes and made my way into the big open parlor where Ryan was. The sound echoed throughout the entire room when I opened the heavy white door to the parlor and closed it behind me. I stood still for a moment to look at Ryan's body, which had been laid peacefully in the front of the room with an American flag hung behind him. The room felt drafty and larger than it actually was as I made my way to the front of it to see my husband. I had been afraid to see him at first because of the condition he'd been in at the time of his death. Thin, sickly, and skeleton-like, so unlike the man I had married. But as I looked down at Ryan's body, I didn't see someone who was sick anymore. His face looked fuller and healthier, his coloring looked normal for the first time in many weeks, and his hair looked thick and healthy and was styled like how he had worn it in life. A velvet cloth was draped over his neck, and I was curious if they had taken that awful tracheostomy out. I moved the cloth aside and found Ryan's neck free of anything besides a small stitch where his trach had been. He looked like Ryan, and I marveled at how beautiful he was one last time. It all still felt like a dream as I traced my fingertips over where his tracheostomy had once been and then over his forehead, across his eyebrows, and down the tip of his nose and lips. My hand landed with the back of it resting on his one cheek like it had many days prior when he lay in a hospital bed. "Hey, babe," I whispered. He looked so peaceful, happy even. I felt an overwhelming sense of calm, even though I knew this would be the last time I would see Ryan on earth. Standing over Ryan's dead body, I suddenly noticed a familiar warmth beside me, and I immediately recognized it as the warmth of Ryan's presence. He was staying beside me in that moment, comforting me and letting me know he was still there, loving me and guiding me. I smiled to myself, leaned over, and kissed his lips one more time. "I love you, and I'll be seeing you, boo," I said as I gently ran my hand through his hair, overcome with the feeling that he would always be with me.

CHAPTER 13

GUARDIAN ANGEL

IT WAS EARLY MORNING ON THE LAST DAY OF JULY 2022, just one week shy of Ryan's four-month deathiversary. I was still in my pajamas and desperately trying to make myself my first cup of coffee of the day when Ryan's mom, Karen, FaceTimed me. My Nespresso machine buzzed in the background as I answered the call. When the video clicked on, there was Louie, Ryan's K9 partner, pacing back and forth. Karen was watching him for two weeks while his new handler was away on a vacation.

* * *

Before Ryan's accident, Louie had been an integral part of our family for close to three years. Jackson and Louie had been born less than a month apart, so they had grown up together. Ryan and Louie had become synonymous with each other. Ryan would often joke that when people came to the station, they would just ignore him and make a fuss over Louie. Ryan had waited eagerly for seven years to get the go-ahead to start Hatboro's first K9 unit. Even before Ryan knew that his dream would become a reality, he spoke with K9 handlers from all across the Philadelphia region about what it took to start a unit, fundraising, the ins and outs of training, and the sacrifices and hard work that went into becoming an extraordinary handler. When Ryan finally got the green light to spearhead Hatboro's first unit, he was ready to go with a proposal he had prepared years prior that had been sitting in a cabinet drawer at the police department. Ryan didn't just have the desire to be any K9 handler; he wanted to become the *best* K9 handler and be highly regarded and respected by the entire K9 community. It wasn't enough for him to be good at it; Ryan wanted to be fucking great at it. And in less than three years, because of his tireless work with Louie, Ryan was able to earn the respect of departments all across the state for his work as a handler. At the time of Ryan's accident in October 2021, Ryan had only just started seeing the fruits of all his dedication and hard work, and I am forever grateful I got to see him live out his dream, even if it was just for a short period of time prior to his death.

After Ryan's accident, I made the heartbreaking decision not to take Louie in as a pet. As devastating as it was to make that decision, it was an easy one to make because Ryan had put his blood, sweat, and tears into training Louie. I didn't want Ryan's hard work to go to waste. Louie was a tried-and-true working dog, and he would never be truly happy as a house pet. I also was keenly aware that any accomplishments Louie had during his career with his new handler would be due in large part to the solid foundation Ryan had established with him.

* * *

"Hey, Lou!" I shouted into my cell phone screen. Then I felt it, that familiar lump, rise to the top of my throat. I had to actively hold back my tears so I wouldn't alarm Jackson, who was excitedly talking into the phone to Louie.

"Louie. That's my doggy! Hi, Louie!" Jackson said happily into my cell phone screen. My heart shattered into a million pieces as Jackson said those words, *my doggy*. And he was right; Louie had been his dog for so long—since he was a baby. It pained me that Jackson didn't truly grasp the concept of time or the situation, as much as I tried to explain it to him. I loved Louie so much, but it was a stab to my heart to see him.

Louie was the living and breathing embodiment of my life with Ryan and my identity as a K9 officer's wife just ten months earlier, before Ryan's accident had completely shattered our hopes and dreams for our family and changed the trajectory of my life forever. Louie was a painful reminder of the woman and wife I had been when Ryan was alive, a woman I was forced to say goodbye to in October of 2021. Seeing him stopped me in my tracks and brought me to tears.

* * *

It was early on a Saturday morning, and the soft light entered through the windows of the kitchen as I stared out into the backyard, listening to the birds chirping and singing as I sipped on my iced coffee. It was summertime, Ryan's favorite season, and the first without him in ten years. Leo was cooing and laughing in his baby swing to my right, and Jackson was happily watching his tablet, sitting in his underwear at the kitchen table and eating cereal.

Ryan had been gone for a couple of months, and we were settling into our new routine as a family of three—my two sweet baby boys and me. Life without Ryan while he was still alive and in the hospital had been chaotic, messy, and depressing. It was as if, during that time, a dark cloud had followed our family everywhere, and there had been no escape from it. The constant not knowing if Ryan would recover and having to see him physically decline and be in pain had been devastating. Then having to watch such a strong, loving, and beautiful man die in such a barbaric way was the single most difficult thing I have ever had to do in my life. This new chapter without Ryan was heartbreaking in its own unique way. At the age of four, Jackson's sense of time was not like an adult's. He still thought Ryan could walk in the door at any second and yell lovingly, "Jack! Jack!"—as much as I explained to him that wasn't possible. He talked about Ryan every day and remembered him vividly, the special things they'd done together and the moments they'd shared. It was simultaneously the most heart-wrenching and heartwarming experience when Jackson spoke of him. Seeing Leo grow and develop into such a sweet and lively baby was painful because I knew how much Ryan had been looking forward to meeting his second son. Every time Leo laughed, smiled with his mouth wide open, kicked his legs excitedly, or interacted with his big brother in such a sweet way was a cruel reminder of all the wonderful moments Ryan was missing out on. Ryan would have loved and cherished Leo. Leo also looked just like Ryan. I believe that because I couldn't have Ryan here with me on earth, Leo was a physical embodiment of his daddy, with the same middle name and all.

With Ryan's death, the dark cloud of the unknown had been lifted. Ryan was finally free. In knowing Ryan was at peace and no longer in pain, there was room for joy, hope, and new beginnings for our boys and me. And in that moment, looking out my kitchen window, sitting in the home we used to share, I couldn't feel anything but gratitude and endless love for Ryan, our guardian angel forever.

EPILOGUE

I AM WRITING THIS EPILOGUE IN THE SAME Starbucks on Main Street in Doylestown where I wrote the introduction. On that day four months ago, I was waiting for the funeral director down the street to text me to let me know Ryan's ashes were ready for me to pick up. Today, I am physically in the same place, but the emotions coursing through me have changed. It is now August 8, 2022—almost ten months since Ryan's accident and four months and one day after his death. Our son Leo turns seven months old today. Jackson, who was three at the time of Ryan's accident, will be four and a half years old this month. Time is passing, and life is evolving.

In the aftermath of Ryan's death, life has taken on a new, beautiful rhythm, new meaning, and new purpose. There is a dull ache in my heart that I will carry, always, because Ryan is missing out on all the beauty this life has to offer—especially seeing our two wonderful boys grow up. And that means I have the responsibility to experience the amazing wonder of this life for both of us.

I am fully aware that after Ryan died, I could have emotionally died with him. In fact, no one would have blamed me for becoming a shell of a person because of all the trauma and grief I had to endure from the time of Ryan's accident until his death. I could have retreated into myself, emotionally shut myself away from the world, and numbed the pain with whatever I could find, just going through the motions of both life and motherhood. But after Ryan died, my own spirit, as well as Ryan's, told me that I had a bigger purpose on this earth, a purpose that had just been ignited because of the unique life experience I had been through and survived.

I knew I couldn't waste a precious second of this life feeling sorry for myself or being full of rage, regret, or despair. Instead, I took all those low-frequency emotions, and I started moving them around in my body like one of those old-fashioned pinball machines—filling my life with intentional movement, activities that bring me joy, and writing this book to help others going through a similar hell. It would have been selfish for me to keep the experiences I went through between my very close family and me because I have learned, by experiencing my own trauma and grief, that the things that happen to us in life aren't just for us. Once we get to a place of peace and understanding, it is our duty and responsibility to share it with the world and to show others that they too can walk, run, and even dance through the fire and darkness and survive—even thrive. I can now say that through Ryan's death as a catalyst for such profound self-discovery, I have never felt more alive or full of joy, peace, love, and hope for the future for myself and my family.

Ryan's death has not hardened me to the world like it could have, but it has actually allowed me to live life more fully, vibrantly, and consciously. It has taught me that we are truly not guaranteed our next breath. Every moment we are alive on this earth is an absolute miracle and not something to take for granted. I am indebted to Ryan for loving me so beautifully that I am still able to feel his love and presence in my everyday life: in the sunrise and sunset, in my boys' smiles, in a leisurely car ride with the windows down and the perfect song playing. I know there is another great love for me to find in my lifetime because of the way Ryan cherished me as his wife with such grace and ease. It has been one of the hardest things to navigate life without him, but having to manage everything by myself and excelling at it has given me strength and confidence I never knew I had inside me. My boys see a happy, healthy, and competent mother despite all the challenges our family has faced. We are settling into our lives as a family of three very imperfectly but with lots of love to go around.

For those of you who are reading this and going through your own trauma or grief, I pray that you give yourself immense grace in the chaos, the mess, and the darkness. It is an impossible place in which to find yourself, but I have learned that you can either let tragedy and death write the story for you and define your future, or you can use these experiences to write your own story, create your own future, and help others with the lessons you have learned and gained through it all.

When you lose someone so integral to your life, it is the ultimate opportunity for personal growth and empowerment.

The beauty of this life is that *you* get to decide what happens next and what kind of legacy you want to leave. Remember that even in the deepest pit of despair and sadness, there is a redemption story waiting for you. I know you may not see it right now, but believe me when I say that life is so damn beautiful.

AKNOWLEDGMENTS

THANK YOU TO EVERYONE WHO REACHED OUT to me since Ryan's accident and shared their own struggles with grief and trauma—Thank you for being vulnerable, for opening up to me about your pain. As I was dreaming about writing this memoir, and during the writing process, your stories were what propelled me to keep going. I wanted to provide a story that I needed when I was going through the worst days of my life, a point of reference for those who truly need it. Thank you all so much for sharing your tragically beautiful stories with me, as this book would not exist without them. I hope this book makes you feel seen and not so alone. Wishing you all hope and peace.

To my sister, Rachel—Thank you for just being wherever I needed you and showing up during the worst parts of the journey. Thank you for being okay with witnessing and sitting with my pain instead of trying to fix it. Thank you for seeing my potential in writing this book, seeing my vision for the future, and supporting me each step of the way. I love you.

To Anthony—Thank you for really seeing me, for knowing my potential, my worth, and my beauty, and for loving me—even all the messy and dark parts. Thank you for allowing me to experience love again in this life and supporting my dreams.

Thank you for loving my boys and for your patience, generosity, and kindness. I still don't know how I got so lucky. I love you.

To Nancy—My friend and soul sister. We have experienced the worst days of our lives together. I know we came into each other's lives so we could go through life's journey together, helping, guiding, and supporting each other as we navigate life without our soulmates. Let's make Ryan and Steve so proud. I love you so much, and I am always here for you.

To the countless others—too numerous to name—who have supported my family and me since Ryan's accident, who have loved us from afar, who have prayed for us, who have sent gifts and food, and who have gone out of their way to make my boys and me feel thought of and taken care of. Thank you from the bottom of my heart.

ABOUT THE AUTHOR

WHITNEY IS FIRST AND FOREMOST A MAMA TO HER two sons, Leo and Jackson, and they live in Doylestown, Pennsylvania. She practiced law for ten years before losing her husband, at which time she decided to follow her new calling to serve others who are also experiencing grief and trauma. She shares the empowering message that there is so much beauty in life, even after losing a loved one.

She is now a certified grief educator through renowned grief expert David Kessler's program and provides grief coaching. Her passion is providing resources, tangible advice, knowledge, and coaching opportunities for those who are ready for their own transformation and growth, even while grieving.

To learn more about Whitney Lyn Allen, please visit
www.whitneylynallen.com.
Connect with Whitney on social media:
https://www.facebook.com/profile.php?id=5517028
http://linkedin.com/in/whitney-lyn-allen-888b34126
Instagram: *@whitneylynallen*
TikTok: *@whitneylynallen*
To contact the author regarding speaking engagements, other
media inquiries, or with any other questions,
please email *whitneylallen12@gmail.com*

Printed in Great Britain
by Amazon

19949084R00088